I enjoy sharing my books as I do my friends, asking only that you treat them well and see them safely home

Ethel Rosen

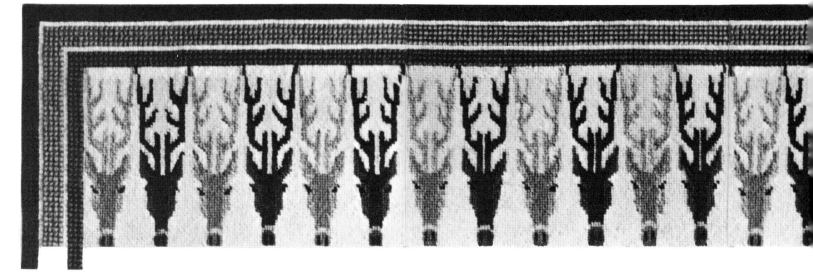

Morton Da Costa's

Designs developed in collaboration with Arne Besser

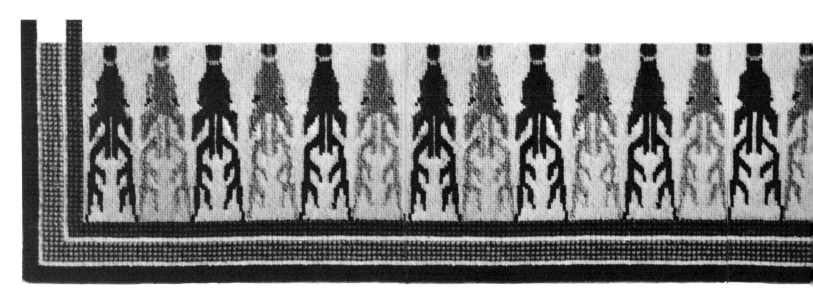

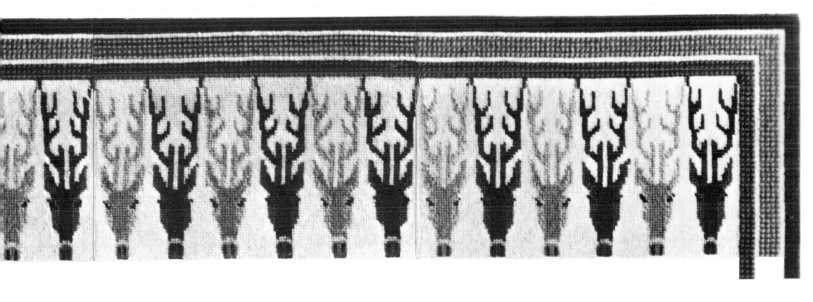

BOOK of
NEEDLEPOINT

SIMON AND SCHUSTER · NEW YORK

Published by Simon and Schuster
Rockefeller Center, 630 Fifth Avenue
New York, New York 10020
Designed by Edith Fowler
Manufactured in the United States of America
1   2   3   4   5   6   7   8   9   10

Library of Congress Cataloging in Publication Data

Da Costa, Morton, 1914-
    Book of needlepoint.

    1. Canvas embroidery—Patterns.   I. Besser,
Arne, illus.   II. Title.
TT778.C3D3   746.4′4   74-11020
ISBN 0-671-21846-8

Acknowledgments

Many thanks are due to many people, especially indulgent friends who, for months, saw only the top of my head as I stitched away in their homes.

There would be no book were it not for the collaboration of my friend Arne Besser, a brilliant artist, who not only lent his expertise to the designs and colors but also undertook the tedious task of drawing the diagrams.

Special thanks to Wynn Hershey for suggesting the lamp project. And to Duke Morell for suggesting the eye chart design. Thanks, too, to Begi Bektesevic for hours of work on the table cover and the rugs.

My deepest gratitude to my sister Isobel for tireless stitching on many of the projects and for typing the manuscript. And to sisters Rita, Lillian, Dorothy and Marion for stitching backgrounds without complaint.

Thanks, too, to Pearl Zion for stitching the chair seat. And, despite the fact that, during the arduous compilation of this book, I was tempted to throttle them, I am finally grateful to Anita Loos for suggesting that I do the book, Ray Pierre Corsini for making it possible, and Diane Harris, my editor, for her sense of humor when mine flagged.

Contents

Preface

Unlike most people who *chose* to take up needlepoint as a rewarding hobby, I was *ordered* to take it up.

Having directed *No Time for Sergeants*, *Auntie Mame*, and *The Music Man* practically within a year's time, I ended up in the hospital with what was diagnosed as nervous exhaustion.

"You're really a nervous disease," my doctor told me.

"Is that merely an observation," I asked, "or something you can prescribe for?"

"Physiotherapy," he replied, "you need some physiotherapy."

"Forget it. I flunked carpentry in high school."

"My wife does needlepoint," he said.

"Good for her!" I answered, marveling at his talent for using the non sequitur.

"She was a nervous disease, too. Needlepoint helped."

All right, so it wasn't a non sequitur. "But she's a woman," I protested.

"Sailors knit," he countered.

The fact that sailors knit was hardly the argument that persuaded me to take up the needle. I desperately wanted to calm down, and since I knew the doctor's wife to be a pretty calm and well-adjusted person, I hoped needlepoint would turn the trick for me too.

When I was released from the hospital, I immediately decided on a project. I instinctively knew there was no incentive in working on something one had no use for. Covering an old footstool that I had planned to have reupholstered seemed a worthy goal. I went to a needlepoint shop, bought half a yard of canvas and some wool and had the saleslady explain the essential stitch—which I later learned was called the Continental stitch. I went home, painted a design on the canvas and, when it was dry, I sat in a large wing chair, in an area that was unfortunately poorly lighted, and began to stitch.

Wonder of wonders, the work did seem to have a calming effect. But it also had a rather frightening side effect.

Of course, the doctor had no way of knowing that, beside being highly strung, I am also highly compulsive. I sat in that wing chair for two days and a night and finished the damned canvas. When I finally stood up, I fell flat on my face due to an extreme case of vertigo, and had to be put away in a dark room for three days.

Now that I was hooked on needlepoint, my next goal was to learn to do it less compulsively. I would decide how much I wanted to accomplish in an evening and not do a stitch more, no matter how much I felt driven to continue. Eventually I could take it in stride, and it ultimately produced the effect the doctor and I both hoped it would. Not only am I as calm as the doctor's wife but, between you and me, I think my work looks a helluva lot better than hers.

I want you to know that when I started, it was not exactly *comme il faut* for a man to do needlepoint. I began by doing it behind closed doors allowing only my family and a few intimate friends to see my handiwork. This caused certain frustrations.

I was going abroad on the *Queen Mary*. I had started a new project: seats and backs for eight dining room chairs. (Fools rush in!) I stitched the designs and farmed out the backgrounds to five sisters, with whom I'm blessed. Wouldn't it be marvelous, I thought, to take a couple of pieces along on my trip and work on them in a deck chair in the sun! But, at that time, the only man who had the guts to needlepoint publicly was the Duke of Windsor. I, alas, being a man addicted to conventional behavior in public, didn't have the nerve to expose my endeavor to the other passengers. Having only the alternatives of disguising myself in a garden hat and a veil or doing the work in my cabin, I chose the latter as the safest.

It happened that one of my sisters was coming back to New York on the return trip of the *Mary*. And, of course, she had the advantage of working on one of the chair backs on the deck, in the sun, with impunity. One day the deck steward who was serving her her morning bouillion pointed to her embroidery and exclaimed, "But, how extraordinary, Madame."

"Oh—do you think it's pretty?" she asked modestly, hoping to imply that she had created the design.

"What I mean is, Madame, there was a gentleman on the trip over who was working exactly the same design."

The fink had obviously snooped around in my cabin and discovered my secret. What's more, he had probably told it to everybody on the ship. So I might just as well have done it on the deck in the sun, in the first place.

Of course, times have changed drastically since I took up the needle. All types of men, including athletes and prize fighters, have not only taken up needlework but are letting the world in on the fact via magazines and television. To name a few, there are former tackle Rosie Grier, prize fighter Rocky Graziano, comedian Arte Johnson, cartoonist Sergio Aragone, to say nothing of house painters, army generals, doctors, and surgeons who claim to do it to keep their fingers nimble. At every Directors' Union meeting I attend, there are at least two or three celebrated members stitching away while conducting the business of the moment.

I, personally, haven't gone so far as to take my work to business meetings, but I do, on occasion, take it along when I'm going to a friend's house for dinner. And, at home, it is no longer possible for me to watch television with my hands folded in my lap. It seems such a waste of time not to be accomplishing something while watching the tube. I simply look at the work when I insert the needle in the canvas and look up at the TV as I'm drawing the wool through. I see more than enough of the programs, believe me.

I feel that it is fortunate that I started doing needlepoint before I ever read a book on the subject. Otherwise, I might never have embarked on what has become an enormously rewarding hobby. I would have been discouraged by the dozens of different stitches contained in most of the books—thinking it necessary to master them all before beginning to work on something. As it turned out, I made some pretty nifty items, knowing how to do only the Continental stitch. Of course, I might have saved myself a lot of tugging and pulling had I known that the Basketweave stitch distorts the canvas less, making the work easier to block. But I learned that, in due time, as I did other stitches, when the need arose. In point of fact, you can accomplish any design on any item never using more than the Continental and Basketweave stitches. Other stitches may be used for variety but, in my estimation, they too often "gild the lily."

There are a sufficient number of books published that are virtually dictionaries of embroidery stitches. I have designed this book to tell you how to make twenty projects, limiting the instruction to exactly what you have to know to finish each one—and no more. I figure that this will be a boon to beginners and might even provide some valuable methods of which even the experienced needlepointer may not be aware.

But, to be frank, the essential motivation for putting this book together is to provide you with the possibility of transferring good designs to canvas, no matter how untalented or inexperienced you are as an artist. The method is simple enough for a child to master. As a matter of fact, most have already mastered it who have done paintings "by the numbers."

No less an important reason for the book is that, with it, there is no need to buy painted canvases, which can be very costly.

The original canvases you buy in shops are, of necessity, expensive, as artists must be employed to paint them by hand. Add to that all the other overhead, and it is not unusual for a painted canvas for a pillow to cost somewhere between forty and sixty dollars. It is hoped that this book will enable you to have a finished project for one quarter of the amount it would cost if you had to buy the painted canvas and have it blocked and finished by a shop.

Another obvious reason for this book is that, prior to its publication, all other books have provided small designs that have to be "blown up" to a larger size to be utilized. This presents a major difficulty for people who are not adept at this technique. Hence, the full-scale tracings and graphs herein provided. The only ability required is to be able to trace and, where graphs are used, to count. You don't even have to paint your canvas if you prefer not to. Merely write the color numbers in the proper areas on your canvas, as given on the tracings, and then stitch these areas with the color of wool indicated for that number on the color chart.

If you follow the steps of each project in sequence as they are described and don't try to take short cuts, you will achieve an easily worked and handsome result.

So, ladies and gentlemen (remember "sailors knit"), get on with it. It's easier than you think.

PART ONE

The Techniques

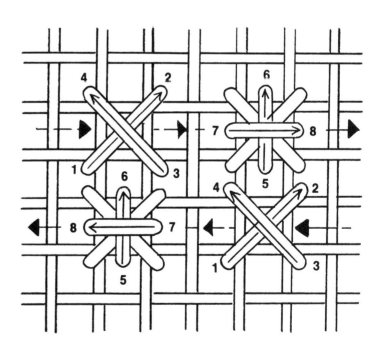

CHAPTER ONE

Pointers on
Alternate Colors and Designs

All of the colors for the projects in this book are specifically indicated with, on occasion, where it is considered feasible, alternate suggestions for those readers who are "color shy" and timid about selecting colors that are not indicated.

Most often, whether you feel you have a strong sense of color or not, you're apt to know what you like when you see it. But how are you to arrive at something you will like that you have not seen? You will obviously know whether you like the colors of the designs as illustrated or whether they will complement the decor in which they are to be used. If you don't like the colors illustrated, or if they won't fit into your decor, how should you proceed?

Let us consider one of the simpler examples: project 18, Rug 2. The colors illustrated are orange, beige and black. You like the design, but you want colors that will reflect the blue-green tones in your upholstery and draperies. So you look at the master color chart and find the alternate colors suggested for an essentially green rug. But, you discover, these are yellow greens that clash with your color scheme. Your next move is to find the blue greens in the master color chart. Pick three of these that have the relative intensity of the colors in the illustrated rug, *e.g.*, a very deep blue green to substitute for the black, one of medium intensity to substitute for the orange and a very light blue green to substitute for the beige —or, if the beige looks well in your decor, retain the beige as the lightest color. This method will give the same design balance as in the illustrated rug, but in your choice of colors.

If your decor is composed essentially of three colors, you might do the rug in those three colors, making sure to simu-

COLOR

late the same intensities—light to dark—of the original design, if you want to retain the same design balance. Let us suppose that your three colors are yellow, lime and white. If you look at the illustrated rug you will discover that the medium shade—orange in this instance—gives the effect of being the dominating color. Decide whether you want yellow, lime or white to predominate in your version. Let us say it is yellow. Yellow, then, will replace the orange in this design. Lime will replace the black; be sure it is of a deeper intensity, or darker, than the yellow. Obviously, your white will replace the beige in the illustrated rug, as it is the lightest color you are going to use.

There is yet another alternative. The whole balance and effect of this design may be altered by making your predominating color the darkest shade. Taking the colors of Rug 2 as an example, where there's orange, use black. Where there's black, use orange, leaving the beige where it is indicated.

If you want the lighter color to predominate, use beige where orange is indicated, and use orange in place of beige, preserving black where it is indicated; or substitute another dark color for the black, such as dark brown or dark green.

The same methods apply to any substitutions you may want to make in other projects.

Don't be afraid of vivid color. The era of "dusty rose" needlepoint is over. A muted decor can be marvelously "punched up" by bright-colored accents of needlepoint in pillows, seat and bench covers, rugs and accessories. As these items are small in scale in comparison to other furnishings, they need real punch to register. My own living room is predominantly putty beige. But character, bite and interest are provided by accents of needlepoint pillows, upholstered seats and accessories in bright tomato reds and acid greens.

It is well to remember, when selecting colors, that the colors of wool seem to end up less intense when worked than they did in the skein, because of the difference in the reflection of light when the stitches are worked flat on the flat plane of the canvas. Consequently, it is wise to choose a color slightly more intense than the color you want to achieve.

Choose colors of varied intensities to give contrast to any project. Using colors of the same intensity will give the finished item an overall dull look.

In choosing a background color, be sure to choose one of sufficient contrast to the design so that the design will be accentuated and featured, unless, of course, you are doing an all-over design and want the subtle effect of, say, a damask. A good rule of thumb in choosing background colors is to choose a bright color for the background of a muted or neutral design and a neutral or light background for a colorful design.

In several of the projects, modeling, or an effect of "roundness" or a sculptured effect is achieved by gradations of color. Let us use a purple plum as an example. If we want to achieve the effect of a plum lying on the canvas with the light source above the canvas, the contour of the plum closest to the light source would get most of the light. This we would stitch in a very pale lavender or even in white. The contours of the plum would get darker as they fell away from the light source. So we would, from the highlight, start grading our colors deeper and deeper, from increasingly darker lavenders to increasingly darker purples. The plum, or any other object so treated, will seem to "stand up" from the canvas. Working the shadow that the plum casts in a muted and darker shade of the background will further heighten the three-dimensional effect.

If your wool shop does not have enough gradations of a color to suit your needs, splitting wools can give you almost twice as many gradations as there are colors available. As will be explained later in greater detail, Persian wools are made up of three plies, or strands, to a thread. These threads are easily separated into their original three plies.

Let us suppose that, to achieve proper modeling for the plum, you need nine shades of purple—graduated from lavender to deep purple—and that your wool shop can provide a gradation of only five colors—lavender to deep purple. If you combine a strand of the lightest lavender with a strand— or two strands—of the next darker shade, you will achieve what seems to the eye an intermediate shade. By continuing to split and blend, you have nine shades.

When you finally decide on your color combination from the chart, hold the actual wools together in the shop to see that they react on each other as you had anticipated. When you see the actual wools together you might want to make some further adjustments in hue and intensity.

Alternate designs for the projects in this book are easily accomplished in two ways.

DESIGN

First, elements from several projects can be extracted and put together to form a new design. From the tracings and graphs provided, on a fresh piece of tracing paper, trace the elements from the different designs that you think might work well together. Each element should be traced on a separate small piece of tracing paper. Now, on a large piece of tracing paper, trace the outer perimeters of the project to be made. Then, move the small-element tracings around on the perimeter tracing until the composition pleases you. Trace the elements onto the perimeter tracing in their proper positions. Go over all the outlines in black ink and you are ready to transfer the new design to canvas, as explained in chapter 4.

Second, if you want totally different designs than those provided for the projects in this book, there is a world of source material that you can use. Designs can be cribbed from greeting cards, museum postcards, art gallery announcements, fabrics, wallpapers, etc., to say nothing of the fact that every library has hundreds of reference books on every period of design and design elements, ancient, classical and modern. The illustrations in children's books are an excellent source. There are also dozens of books with full color renderings of cultivated and wild flowers, fruits and berries, to say nothing of birds, animals, insects, etc. A few styles of letters of the alphabet and numbers are herein provided, but you can find books on lettering that will give you dozens more.

Once you have found the design you want to use, the easiest way to get it onto your canvas is to have it photostated.

Let us assume that you've found in a department store catalog a picture of a scarf that has on it a handsome unicorn in a garden of stylized flowers. You'd like to use this design on the sixteen-inch pillow project. But the picture measures only two inches square.

Look in the classified section of your phone directory under Photo Copying and find a laboratory near you that does photostating. Take your catalog photo to the lab and tell them you want it blown up to fourteen-by-fourteen inches, or seven times the size of the photo of the scarf. This will leave an inch free of design on all four sides of a sixteen-inch pillow. Tell the lab that you want a positive print. You will receive a black-and-white print of the design to your scale. If the original picture you gave them was in color, the colors will show up on your photostat as various shades of gray. Lay a piece of tracing paper over this and draw from it the outlines you need for the design, simplifying the design wherever you think it necessary. Referring to the original color photo, draw in the lines you need to indicate the demarcations of color areas. Go over the tracing in black ink so that it will show through the canvas when you transfer it.

If the photostat was made from a simple line drawing, you may not need the intermediate tracing but may be able to trace from the photostat directly to the canvas.

Photostating can be used not only to enlarge but to reduce. And you may have elements from several different designs photostated to use together in one design of your own. If one element of your source design is four inches and you need it to be half that size in your new design, ask the lab to reduce it to two inches. It will be obvious to you that when photostats are enlarged or reduced, the relative proportions of length to width of the original must remain the same.

Now that you have all of the elements you need in their proper sizes, shift them about on a perimeter tracing, as explained above.

The method of transferring the design to your canvas and of indicating color is discussed in chapter 4.

CHAPTER TWO

The Materials

CANVAS Needlepoint canvas comes in many qualities, woven out of cotton, flax, hemp or linen. It is made up of threads which form square holes, all exactly the same size if it is a good canvas. I suggest that the time and effort you are going to invest in each project deserves the best quality of canvas available to you. That means a tightly woven canvas in which the meshes are even and will not shift—even as the canvas loses its sizing. Be sure, too, that you are buying a canvas that has the same number of meshes per inch both horizontally and vertically. Against a ruler, count the meshes in one inch in both directions to be sure they are the same. This test is especially important when the canvas is to be used for working geometric designs.

You can obtain needlepoint canvas in several widths—usually 24-inch, 36-inch, 40-inch, 54-inch—and some rug canvases come in even wider widths, but they are usually difficult to find.

The number of threads per inch in the canvas determines how large your stitches will be. A rug canvas that will accommodate very large stitches has three threads per inch and is known as a #3 canvas. Any canvas up to seven threads per inch (or a #7 canvas) is usually called rug or "quickpoint" canvas. Canvas that has anywhere from eight threads per inch (#8 canvas) to 18 threads per inch (#18 canvas) will produce *gros point*. Canvases that have twenty threads or more to the inch will produce stitches small enough to be called *petit point*. Gros point and petit point are both worked in the same way. Their names merely reflect the size of the stitch.

Naturally, the smaller the stitch, the longer it takes to complete a project. The canvas most often used is #10. It works up rather quickly and allows one to achieve sufficient detail to be effective. Finer canvases must be used for more detail; consequently, the subject matter of the design indicates the mesh size of the canvas to be used.

I have included designs for rug canvas projects (usually for a #5 canvas) for those who like to see quick results. Most of the other projects are designed for canvas ranging from #10 to #16 so that more detail can be achieved and yet not be overly taxing.

Canvas can be obtained in either single or double mesh. The single-mesh is called mono canvas and is formed by crossing one warp thread with one woof thread. This canvas usually comes in white and is easy to paint designs on.

The double-mesh canvas, known as penelope canvas, is woven with two warp threads and two woof threads for each intersection.

The advantage of penelope canvas is that, whereas you can stitch over each double thread intersection as if it were mono canvas, you can also split each intersection into four smaller stitches by merely separating the double threads. Consequently, using a #10 penelope canvas, you can do the design in petit point for greater detail, using twenty stitches to the inch, and the background in gros point, using ten stitches to the inch.

Mono Canvas (Single Mesh)

Penelope Canvas (Double Mesh)

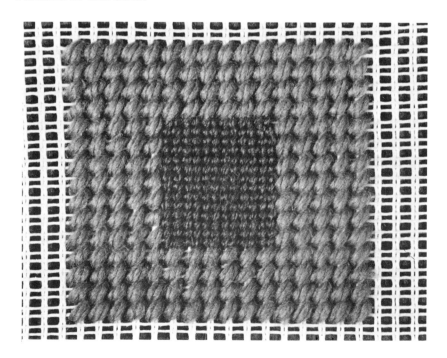

Petit point and gros point worked on the same piece of penelope canvas.

Because of the double threads, it is sometimes confusing to count stitches on penelope canvas. It is also easier to make mistakes on it as you can often unwittingly put your needle between the double threads instead of the holes that they circumscribe. For these reasons, I have used mostly mono canvas for the projects. In each instance the number of the canvas to be used is indicated, as well as the most economical width and yardage required.

YARN Persian wool is the most versatile kind of wool for needlepoint and comes in a very wide range of colors with many gradations of hues. It is made up of three plies, or strands, loosely twisted together to form a thread. The strands are easily separated so that you may use one, two, or three strands, depending on the demands of the canvas. I recommend the following to cover the canvas properly and yet not overcrowd it:

For #10 canvas	use full three-strand thread
For #12 and #14 canvas	use two strands
For #16 and #18 canvas	use one strand

For rug canvas use rug wool—a thicker three-ply wool that is used for #5 mesh canvas or coarser. However, if your shop does not carry rug wool, you can double up on the three-strand Persian wool described above.

For #7 canvas	use two full threads (six strands)
For #5 canvas	use two full threads plus two strands or a total of eight strands.

All of the projects in this book are worked with three-ply Persian needlepoint wools or three-ply Persian rug wools. The amount needed is indicated for each project. But no amount under one eighth of an ounce is specified as it is doubtful that you can buy less than that amount.

Since the kinds of Persian wool most often carried in needlepoint shops are two brands called Paterna and Paragon, I have used the colors available in both brands for the master color chart. Also, for your convenience, I have included tables that give the Paterna and Paragon color numbers comparable to my color chart numbers. If your shop carries another brand, merely choose colors closest to the ones called for on my color chart.

Needlepoint needles have large eyes and blunt points. They vary in size, to be used for different sized meshes. The more meshes per inch, the finer the needle must be. The needles are numbered—their numbers and uses follow:

#21 to 24	for petit point
#18 to 20	for gros point (#18 is most commonly used for #10 to #14 canvases)
#15	for #7 and #8 canvas
#13	for rug canvases

You may need some or all of the following materials. It is well to have them all on hand.

Light gray indelible marker
Black indelible marker
Tracing paper
Rabbit-skin glue
Brown wrapping paper
Sponge
Hand steamer
Sobo glue
One-inch-wide masking tape
Piece of plywood for blocking
Rustproof tacks or pushpins
Small scissors
Carpet thread
Latch hook
Mercerized thread

Other materials needed for preparing and finishing certain projects are listed in the instructions for those specific projects.

CHAPTER THREE

The Stitches

Following are the instructions for the stitches needed to work every project in this book. Instead of trying to master them all at once, select a project and learn only the stitch or stitches it calls for. In this way you will only have to learn one or two stitches at a time. You will learn the others as subsequent projects are chosen.

All the needlepoint stitches, no matter what method you use to work them, are diagonal stitches that cover one intersection of threads. When the canvas is held so that the cut edges are at the top and bottom and the selvages run vertically at the sides, the direction of the diagonal of the stitch never varies, slanting always from lower left to upper right.

Note that when you turn your canvas around so that the top becomes the bottom, these stitches will still be slanting in the same direction. When instructed to turn the canvas upside down, you must turn it *completely* upside down, not halfway round, so that what was the upper right-hand corner of the canvas becomes the lower left-hand corner.

The difference between the Continental stitch and the Basketweave stitch is only in the way in which it is worked. The stitches look the same on the surface of the canvas. They look quite different on the back of the canvas.

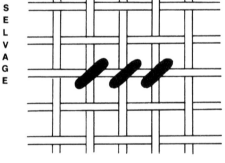

Direction of the slant of all needlepoint stitches.

Left, back of canvas worked in Continental stitch;

Right, back of canvas worked in Basketweave stitch.

This stitch is convenient when used to outline areas that will later be filled with the Basketweave stitch, and whenever a single line of stitching is needed. Try not to use this stitch in large areas, as it has the disadvantage of distorting the canvas, making it more difficult to block.

The Continental stitch is always worked from right to left. Pull the needle and yarn up through the hole below and to the left of the intersection of threads you want the first stitch to cover. Then insert the needle in the hole above and to the right of the intersection you want to cover. Pull the stitch flat (don't yank), and you have made your first Continental stitch. Now bring the needle up again through the hole immediately to the left of the hole in which you started your first stitch, and put your needle down through the hole to the left of the hole that completed your first stitch. You have completed your second stitch. Continue this sequence until you have gone as far to the left as your design or background indicates. (As you become confident about the placement of the stitches, you will find it easier to draw the needle through two holes at once, thus keeping your hand always on the top of the canvas.)

To make your next row of stitches, turn the canvas *completely* upside down and, working from right to left again, work your second row of stitches exactly as you did the first. When you have completed that row, turn your canvas right side up and work the third row and so on.

Sometimes, you will find it necessary to work this stitch in a straight or irregular vertical line or a diagonal line. In that instance, instead of working from right to left, you work from top to bottom.

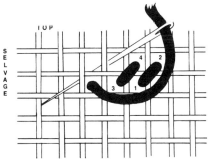

1

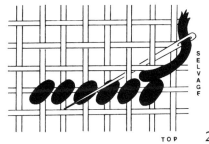

2

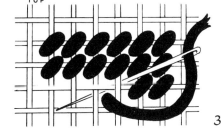

3

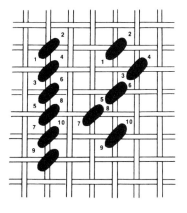

Working the Continental stitch in a straight or irregular vertical line.

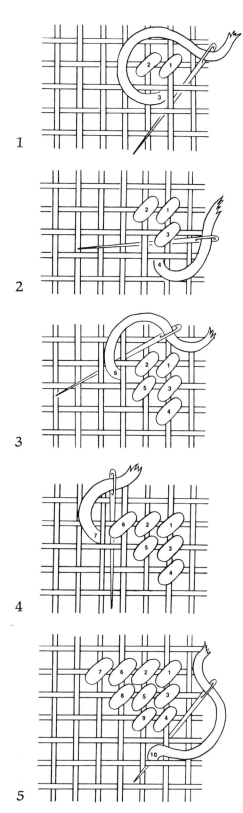

This stitch is so named because of the basketweave pattern it makes on the back of the canvas. Its main advantage is that it distorts the canvas very little, making it easy to block. Its closely woven backing makes it particularly sturdy for rugs and upholstered pieces that get a lot of use. Another advantage of this stitch is that you don't have to keep turning the canvas to work it as you do with the Continental stitch. It is hard to use this stitch for outlining a design or where there are very small or intricate motifs. For those, use the Continental stitch. But, wherever an area is large enough to allow it (about an inch square), use the Basketweave stitch.

At the top right-hand corner of the area to be worked, make two Continental stitches. Instead of continuing to the left horizontally, bring the needle up through the hole directly under the hole you started with and insert it one hole above and to the right. Your work now looks like this:

Under this third stitch, make a fourth stitch, bringing your needle out in the hole that will allow you to make the fifth stitch to the left of stitch #3.

You are now working upward, toward the top of the canvas and will notice that when working stitches that are climbing up the diagonal, the needle is horizontal.

Stitch #6 is worked next to stitch #2.

You have now arrived back at the top of your work.

Work one stitch to the left of stitch #6, bringing your needle out of the hole next to stitch #5. You are now descending the diagonal and will note that, whereas all the stitches ascending the diagonal are made with the needle in a horizontal position, all the stitches made descending the diagonal are made with the needle in a vertical position. Continue the descending stitches until you have completed stitch #10.

After you have inserted the needle to complete stitch #10, bring it out in the hole below the bottom hole of stitch #10. Note that the stitch at the bottom of a diagonal row and the stitch at the top of a diagonal row are the only ones made with the needle in a slanting position.

This puts you in position to start ascending your diagonal with a horizontal needle for stitch #11, as for stitch #4.

Remember, as you get to the top of the work, make one stitch to the left of the completed row (with a slanted needle) to put you in position to descend the diagonal with a vertical needle.

Sometimes the contours of a design make it difficult to reach all the edges of the design with the Basketweave stitch. Merely fill in the random stitches that the diagonal line has missed with Continental stitches. You will also sometimes find that turning the canvas upside down makes it easier to get at an area in order to work the Basketweave stitch.

Often, as in the case of backgrounds, you will have to split up your work areas to avoid working across the entire design. Thus, you will be working the background areas in sections. When you join two areas of Basketweave, be sure to look at the back of the work first. If the last diagonal row of stitches you worked made horizontal stitches on the back of the canvas, your new row should be started at the top, working down to make vertical stitches on the back of the canvas, crossing the existing horizontal ones. Or, conversely, if your last row of stitches on the back of the canvas was vertical, start at the bottom and work up, making horizontal stitches on the back to crisscross the vertical ones already there. If you are careless in this and make two rows of ascending horizontal stitches next to each other or two rows of descending vertical stitches next to each other, the basketweave pattern on the back of the canvas will be interrupted and may show on the face of the canvas as a depressed ridge. *To avoid this flaw,* follow this procedure: If, whenever you start a new area of Basketweave, you make it a point to make stitch #1 across an intersection where the crosswise (or horizontal) thread is on top, all the areas of Basketweave will come together properly, horizontal rows alternating with vertical. However, if you forget to do this, it is better to stop short of joining two areas of Basketweave stitch that look as though they will come together improperly; instead fill in the blanks with the Continental stitch. The area of Basketweave and the area of Continental will differ in thickness, but there won't be the pronounced ridge that occurs when two rows of horizontal stitches or two rows of vertical stitches are adjacent.

This stitch is particularly valuable when one thread of three-ply yarn does not sufficiently cover the canvas. This is especially likely when using rug yarn on a #3 rug canvas.

I have also used it for variety, sometimes, to give a "bump" stitch effect and for raised borders.

Work the stitch from right to left, as you do with the

THE CROSS STITCH

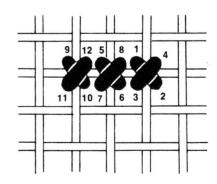

Continental stitch, and complete each cross as you proceed.

Make sure the top stitch of each cross always slants in the same direction—from lower left to upper right.

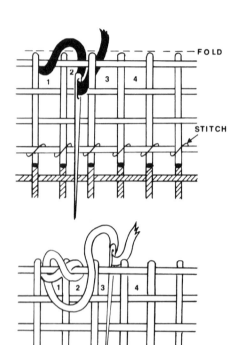

THE BRAID STITCH This stitch is used as a decorative finish for the edges of a single piece of canvas—as for a belt—or to join two pieces of canvas together to make an envelope—as for an eyeglass case. It is also used to join flat pieces of canvas together where the join is part of the design, as in the Tile Design rugs.

The stitch is worked over a folded edge of canvas.

Preparing the canvas for a finished edge is explained in chapter 4.

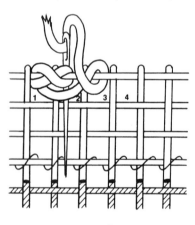

To work a Braid stitch edging on a single piece of canvas with a hemmed edge, hold the canvas with the *wrong* side facing you. Secure your yarn under the stitches near where you are going to start. You will be working from *left* to *right*.

Insert the needle from the right side of the canvas (the side away from you) and, with the needle pointing toward you, work two stitches over the fold, filling two holes.

Now come through the first hole again, needle pointing toward you and, going over the fold of the canvas, bring it out again toward you, through the third hole.

Go over the fold again and bring the needle out toward you through the second hole again.

Go over the fold again and bring your needle out through the fourth hole.

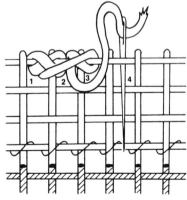

Continue to work in this way, forming a braided edge. You will notice that you are alternately progressing one hole and backing up one hole. Always remember to throw the wool over the edge of the canvas and always insert your needle into the side of the canvas away from you. When you've run out of thread, bring the end to your side of the canvas and pass it through several stitches to the left. Cut off the excess. Now, securing the new thread under the same stitches on your side of the canvas, bring the thread out toward you, one stitch short of the end of the previously finished work. Throw the yarn over the canvas and come out the next empty hole to the right. You are now ready to continue.

When edging a rectangle, continue to work continuously, the way you have been, right around the corners and along the next side.

When you have finished braiding the perimeter and arrived at the place you started, continue to make a few stitches over your first two stitches to complete the work.

To bind two pieces of canvas together, both pieces must be prepared for a finished edge. First whip them together, wrong sides facing each other, with carpet thread, the two pieces matched hole for hole. Now work the braid stitch over the two edges as if you were working over one edge. You can start by securing your yarn in the back of the needlepoint of one of the pieces, bringing your yarn out between the two pieces you are stitching together.

Binding two pieces of work together with the Braid stitch.

Penelope canvas will accommodate your design in small stitches, for greater detail, and allow you to stitch your background in larger stitches, to be worked more quickly.

Penelope canvas can be obtained in many mesh sizes. A 10/20 canvas will allow you to do twenty small stitches to the inch and ten large stitches to the inch. An 8/16 canvas allows sixteen small stitches to the inch and eight large stitches to the inch.

Before working your small stitches, separate the vertical threads as shown below. The stitches are worked over the intersections as shown in the same diagram.

The background stitches are worked over the double-mesh intersections as shown below:

Sometimes there will be single threads of canvas exposed between the small stitches of the design and the larger stitches of the background. Merely cover these with small stitches in the background color.

*STITCHING
PENELOPE CANVAS*

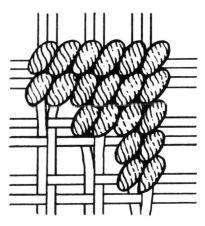

Separating threads and working penelope canvas with petit point.

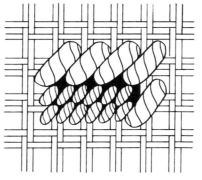

Working both petit point and gros point on penelope canvas.

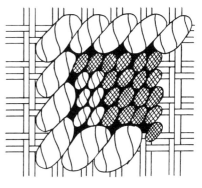

Covering exposed threads with background color.

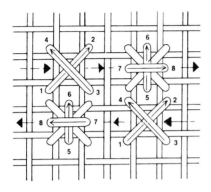

I include this stitch because it is useful in making handsome texturized borders, like the one used on the Backgammon Board, project 12. The effect is that of a series of three-dimensional bumps.

The stitch may be worked left to right or right to left without turning the canvas. When planning an area of Double Cross stitch, be sure you have an even number of horizontal threads and vertical threads, as each stitch uses two of each.

As diagrammed, make the diagonal cross first, then the vertical-horizontal cross. Be sure that all the strokes in each Double Cross stitch are worked in the same order, and, especially, that the final stitch is the horizontal one.

CHAPTER FOUR

Preparing the Canvas
and Transferring the Design

Some projects in this book require joining two pieces of canvas together invisibly where canvas of sufficient width is not available for the project. This technique is explained in chapter 9 and in the project instructions where it applies. The method is called "grafting."

Other projects require hemming the canvas for a finished edge. This process is described later in this chapter.

For some pillows and similar projects where no special preparation is required, it is still necessary to bind the cut edges of the canvas to keep them from raveling as you work.

Start with a piece of canvas large enough to leave at least a two-inch margin of unworked canvas on all sides of the design. This margin will be used later to facilitate blocking. Also, for ease in blocking, always work on a rectangular piece of canvas, even if your design is oval, circular or eccentric in shape.

Selvage edges do not need binding. To bind the cut edges, fold strips of one-inch-wide masking tape over each, so that there will be at least a half-inch on the face and a half-inch on the back of the canvas.

With the selvages running vertically, mark the top of the canvas with your indelible marker. Also, on the front and back of the canvas, mark the center of each of the four sides as registry marks to be used when you are blocking.

Now, on a piece of paper about four inches wider and four inches longer than your canvas, draw the exact outline of the full piece of canvas you're using (not the outline of the design) and extend the registry marks from the middle of each side of the canvas to each side of the drawing on the paper. I find that brown wrapping paper is best for this purpose. Put this paper pattern aside to be used when blocking.

PREPARING THE CANVAS FOR A FINISHED EDGE

Several projects in this book require that a hem of from four to six meshes deep be turned back before the needlepoint is started. These hems should be folded carefully so that the holes in the hem and the holes on the right side of the canvas are in perfect register.

First, run a fine line of a white, invisibly drying glue, like Sobo, along each cut edge of the canvas and allow it to dry. Now fold the hem back, on the fourth mesh for penelope canvas and between the fifth and sixth meshes of regular mono needlepoint canvas. When using penelope canvas, fold on a double thread. When using mono canvas, fold between two threads so your edge will be made up of two threads—one on each side of the fold.

These double threads on the edge are required for working the Braid stitch, described in chapter 3. Sew the hems down along the cut edge of the hem, using a backstitch. In the case of a penelope rug canvas, if the canvas is folded carefully, it is possible to sew the hems down on a sewing machine—setting the machine for twelve stitches to the inch and running the line of stitches between the double threads on the cut edge of the canvas.

When preparing the canvas, as above described, for a finished edge, don't worry about the added double thickness of the hem and the four thicknesses of the canvas in the corners. Work over the hems as if they were a single layer of canvas, and the added thickness will not be apparent in the finished work.

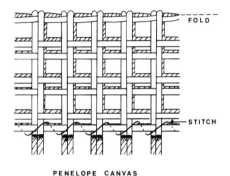

PENELOPE CANVAS

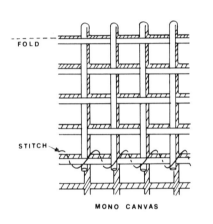

MONO CANVAS

TRANSFERRING THE DIAGRAM OF THE DESIGN TO THE CANVAS

For many of the projects included in the book, it is necessary to transfer the outlines and color areas of the designs, provided in full scale for you on tracing paper, to your canvas. One of the easiest ways to do this is to use a window as an improvised tracing table. With masking tape, attach the project tracing to the window. Again with masking tape, attach your piece of canvas to the window, over the tracing, matching any registry marks. The black lines of the design tracings will now be clearly seen through the canvas. Trace the design onto the canvas with a light or medium shade of gray or blue indelible marker. Avoid the use of darker markers as they may show through your finished work. And be absolutely sure that the marker you use is *indelible*, or it will bleed onto the wools during the blocking or cleaning of the finished work. Even if the marker is marked "indelible," it is wise to test it with water to make sure the claim is true.

If you have a glass-topped table, you may find it more convenient to use than the window. Merely put a lamp on the floor below the table so that the light will shine up through the tracing and canvas.

Bolder and less intricate designs may show through the canvas sufficiently to trace if you simply put a piece of white paper under the tracing on a regular table with an opaque surface.

It is not necessary to paint your canvas. Once you have selected the colors of the wools indicated for the project, put each color in a separate envelope, marked with the color chart number that corresponds to that color. Now, when an area is marked #29, you work that area with strands of wool taken from the #29 envelope. By using this procedure, you are virtually "painting" your canvas with wool.

If, however, you decide to paint in the color areas of the tracing, the best medium to use is acrylic paints. These are water soluble, but they dry absolutely indelibly and will not "bleed" when the canvas is blocked or cleaned. They are easy to use and have the advantage over oil paints of drying quickly. Use the paints sufficiently thin so that they don't block up the holes in your canvas, and yet not so thin that they will penetrate the canvas and dissolve the sizing.

In mixing your paints, match the colors to the colors that are indicated on the color chart. If, let us say, several areas are marked with the number 29, refer to the color chart and mix your paint to match #29. Paint that color in all the areas on your canvas that are marked #29. Now mix another color called for, and paint in all the areas of that color. In other words, paint "by the numbers." Continue mixing paint and filling in areas until the entire design is painted.

WORKING FROM GRAPHS

Some projects are more easily translated into graphs than into tracings. In such instances, full-scale graphs are supplied. Although when working from a graph you have to keep referring to it and counting, it is, nevertheless, easy to read.

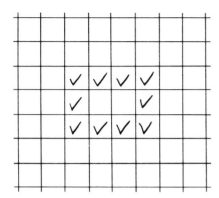

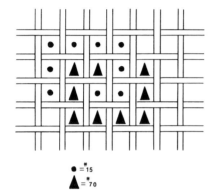

● = #15
▲ = #70

In the graphs for needlepoint, each square represents one stitch.

In the diagram at left, an oblong is represented that is made up of three stitches by four stitches.

To indicate the color of each needlepoint stitch, symbols are used. These merely indicate change of color, not change of stitch. The symbols and the colors they represent are printed in the lower diagram.

The graph for the design of two overlapping oblongs requires you to make a stitch in #15 red, wherever the symbol ● appears and a stitch in #70 black, wherever the symbol ▲ appears. There will be as many symbols used as there are colors in the design.

When working from graphs it is often helpful to mark guidelines on the canvas. A line marking the center of the work, both horizontally and vertically, will make counting and orientation easier. When working on a project such as the lamp base, you might find it helpful to draw lines indicating the width of each design band.

CHAPTER FIVE

Pointers on Work Habits to Develop

Don't work with too long a piece of yarn as it will become frayed by constant pulling through the abrasive edges of the canvas mesh. The best length to use is about eighteen or twenty inches.

To thread your needle, fold the end of your yarn over the pointed end of the needle, pinching the thread close to the needle between your thumb and forefinger. Withdraw the needle and push the pinched fold through the eye of the needle.

 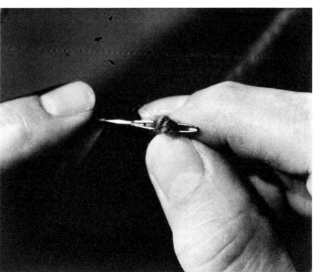

To start your work, on the front of the canvas put your needle into a hole six or eight holes below where you want your first stitch to be. Now bring your needle out at the hole where you

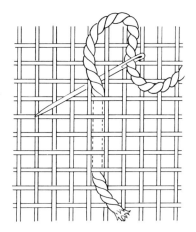

Starting a thread.

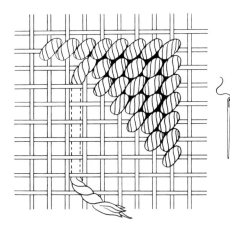

Finishing a thread.

want to start your first stitch, drawing your yarn through until just a small tail remains on the front of the canvas.

Now, as you work, you will be covering the thread on the back of the canvas, thus securing it. When your stitching reaches the little tail left on the face of the canvas, merely snip the tail off. You can work the entire canvas this way, making it unnecessary ever to turn to the back of it to secure threads—either when beginning a thread or ending one. To use this method to finish off a thread, when you've finished your stitch to the back of the canvas bring your needle and yarn out six to eight holes below your last stitch, removing the needle and leaving a tail of yarn.

The yarn left on the back of the canvas will be worked over and secured by subsequent stitches. Merely cut off the tails as the new stitches reach them.

The other method of starting a thread is to pass it through six or eight existing stitches on the back of the canvas. When you come to the last few inches of yarn, turn your canvas over and weave it through the last six or eight stitches you worked. Be sure to clip off excess bits of yarn on the back of your canvas after you have secured it through several stitches, as loose ends tend to get caught up in your subsequent work and appear on the face of the canvas.

Don't stitch too tightly. If you do, you will distort the canvas needlessly and your stitches will not have the nice rounded contour that they should and, consequently, not cover as well. As you draw your thread through when making a stitch, stop pulling as soon as the stitch is easily formed and is flat to the canvas. Don't *tug*.

Your yarn will get twisted as you stitch. Periodically, turn your canvas upside down, allowing the yarn and needle to dangle. The yarn will then untwist itself. Overly twisted yarn becomes thin, and consequently it doesn't cover the canvas as well and makes the work look uneven.

Because the canvas is made up of squares, you will not always be able to stitch a curved line or a diagonal line as it is drawn. To achieve a curved line, you will sometimes have to work a stitch outside the line or inside it, depending only on your judgment. Don't let this worry you. The effect to the eye will still be a smooth curve.

Often, to achieve the effect of a straight diagonal line, you will have to work it in a series of "steps"—but the effect to the eye will be that of a straight line.

Weave a few threads of each color into the back of your work in case you ever have to mend it. These threads will go through the same processes of blocking and cleaning that the rest of the canvas goes through, so they will always match their counterpart colors in the finished piece.

I believe that every piece should be signed or initialed and that the date the work was finished should be incorporated. There are two ways this can be done.

1. Draw the monogram and date in a corner of your canvas and work it as you would any other part of the design.

2. After the entire piece is finished, work with cotton or silk floss over existing stitches in the background to form your initials and the date. This method can also be used to intensify highlights and shadows, or other details, after the work is finished.

If you have worked some areas too tightly and the canvas shows through, you may correct this in one of two ways:

1. Using thin acrylic paints of the proper colors and a fine brush, carefully "paint out" the white canvas threads where they show through.

2. Using one or two plies of the proper color, work over the stitches that were pulled too tightly.

You can conserve wool by working a strand to the end, even though you've completed the area of that color. For example, if you have finished an area of a color and still have a reasonable length of that color left in your needle, cross over to another area needing that color, if it is not too far away, and work it with the yarn you have left in the needle. If there is already some stitched work between these two areas, on the back of the canvas pass the thread you are using to bridge those areas through the stitches of the finished work. If the trip from one area to another is longer than an inch and a half, it is better to lock off the strand and start anew on the new area.

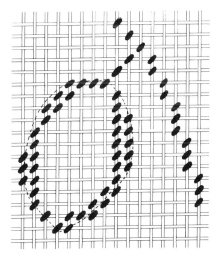

Simulating curves.

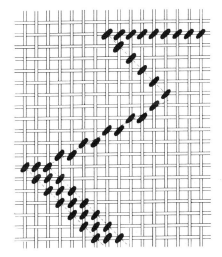

Simulating diagonal lines.

If you want to take out one or more of the stitches you have just worked, *don't* try to shove the threaded needle back through the hole. It will split threads and become entangled. Unthread your needle and pull the stitches out with the blunt end of your needle. Rethread the needle and continue to work. If you want to redo a mistake in a completed part of the canvas, cut one of the stitches carefully, then rip out a sufficient number of stitches to give you about two and a half inches of yarn on each side of the mistake. Thread each end and weave it into the back of the canvas to secure it. Now, with a new piece of yarn, secured on the back, rework the area you have ripped.

Wash your hands before you start to stitch in order to keep your work clean. If, despite your efforts, the work becomes soiled, clean it before blocking by laying it on a flat surface and spraying it with a dry cleaner from a spray can, wiping it with a soft cloth, or by gently going over it with an upholstery foam cleaner and a sponge. Use a light hand so as not to pull up nubs or flatten the wool too much. Do *not* immerse the piece in water as this will wash out the sizing of the canvas and make the piece hard to handle.

Where pieces of needlework are to be sewn together by hand or by sewing machine, as in the case of the vest or a pillow, make sure that the cut edges of the canvas to be used in the seams have been treated with a white glue, such as Sobo, to keep the seams from fraying out as the piece is used. Run a thin line of the glue along the last mesh of the canvas and allow to dry.

CHAPTER SIX

Pointers on Blocking

Blocking is necessary for every needlepoint project. The general way to block is discussed here. Variations are sometimes given under specific projects.

Even with the Basketweave stitch, there is bound to be some distortion of the canvas. It is always necessary to bring the canvas back to its true rectangular shape before finishing it. This is achieved by blocking. Note that, even if the perimeter of your project is circular, oval or eccentric in shape, you always work it on a rectangular piece of canvas for blocking. You don't cut away the excess until after the piece has been blocked.

I use a piece of plywood as a blocking board. You may use a breadboard, if you like, or any piece of wood you don't mind putting tack holes into.

To the board I tack the piece of brown wrapping paper that has the outline on it of the piece of canvas I started with before stitching. I make sure the corners of this pattern are absolutely square by using a carpenter's right angle.

Now lay your finished work, face *down,* on the paper pattern. Tack down the top edge of the canvas, matching the center registry mark on your canvas to the center registry mark on the paper pattern. Use stainless upholstery tacks or stainless pushpins. You may use a staple gun, if you prefer, but make sure the staples are steel ones that do not rust.

Place the tacks in the unworked canvas, about one half inch in from the edge, at one-half or three-quarter inch intervals. Now, matching registry marks on the left side, pull the canvas until you can tack down the left side to its proper place on the paper pattern. Then, pulling as you go, tack down the

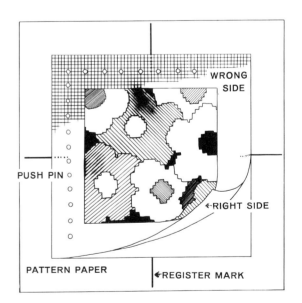

Blocking a piece of finished work.

right side to its outline on the pattern. If you're having difficulty, steam the work with a hand steamer or a steam iron. The hand steamer may be placed against the canvas, but a steam iron should be held about two inches above the canvas so that it doesn't flatten your stitches too much.

After applying steam, pull the canvas again, repeating this process until you are able to pull the work into its proper pattern. I have found a pair of pliers useful when the canvas is stubborn.

Finally, tack down the bottom edge, making sure the registry mark matches that on the paper pattern.

After the work is completely tacked down on all four sides and exactly matches the paper pattern, go over the canvas again with a generous application of steam. I find the hand steamer (the one sold for use on clothing) much more convenient than a steam iron. It works faster, too, as it can be held right up against the work.

Allow your blocked piece to dry thoroughly for at least twenty-four hours, but do not remove it from the blocking board at the end of that time. No matter how carefully a piece is blocked and how well it is steamed, it will eventually creep back into at least part of its original distortion. In order to prevent this, a glue or sizing should be applied.

From an art supply store, obtain rabbit-skin glue. This comes in the form of granules. Put two tablespoons of the granules in a clean, one-quart glass jar, and fill the jar with water. Over a lighted burner, place the jar in a saucepan half-filled with water. Keep stirring the contents of the jar until the granules are completely melted. Remove the jar from the stove and allow it to stand until it is cool enough to handle.

Dip a sponge in the solution and wet the back of your canvas with it, using enough to penetrate through the stitches on the back of the canvas, but not so much as to penetrate to the wool stitches on the face of the canvas. Allow this to dry for at least forty-eight hours.

When the canvas is completely dry, you may remove the tacks and take the work up from the blocking board.

Your stitches will look far more even than when you worked them, and the piece will not lose its shape.

Never push pins into finished needlepoint. When you are blocking canvas that has been prepared for finished edges, put the pins into the space between the finished work and the canvas thread along the prepared edge.

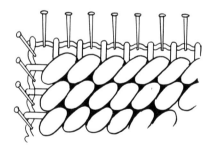

Placing the pins when blocking the finished edge.

It is a good idea, after the work has been blocked, to spray the right side with a soil resister, such as Scotchgard. Spray it *lightly* four or five times, being sure not to saturate the stitches, so the solution rests on top of them.

Of course, you can have your work blocked professionally, but with very little trouble you can save a lot of money by doing it yourself.

CHAPTER SEVEN

Borders and Lettering

You may want to dress up a project by placing a border around it, or by putting a message or a monogram somewhere on the work. For that reason, I have included, at the end of this chapter, graphs for several decorative borders and alphabets. Also provided are several "shields" in which monograms may be placed.

Several borders may be used together, one within the other, to make handsome "frames" around your work. Be sure, when you decide to add a border to a design, that you leave sufficient canvas for it.

The borders are made up of repeat patterns. Always start the work on borders by placing one full repeat pattern in the center of the top. Now work to the right as far as you want the border to extend, making sure you end with a full repeat. Now, work the left half of this border with the same number of repeats as the right. Put in a corner motif at the right end and at the left end. Now, from the end of this border, work down one of the sides, as far as you want it to extend, making sure you end with a full repeat and a corner motif. You can now work the other two sides, copying the finished work.

Work the same way when putting borders within borders. I find it easiest to work out the placement of motifs within a border by stitching the innermost border first.

When using a monogram of two or three letters, count the number of stitches the combination will use, both vertically and horizontally, including spaces. Let us say that the monogram will cover 30 stitches horizontally and 10 stitches vertically. Find the center of the area where you want to put the monogram. Count 15 stitches on each side of the center mark and 5 stitches above it and 5 stitches below it. Now draw an oblong box, determined by these marks, and work your letters within it.

When working a whole legend in letters, be sure to count the entire number of stitches it will cover, including spaces. Find the center of the area where it is to be worked and then count off, to the left, half the number of meshes to be used in the legend. This will give you your starting point.

When using one of the shields to place a monogram in, try elongating or shortening part of the letters to conform to the contours of the shield.

Following are some borders, alphabets and shields you might find useful for projects in this book or for other projects not contained herein.

Note: More borders may be lifted from project 13. Corner motifs are provided on the graph for that project in case you want to use the bands on the lamp base as borders.

Alphabet 1

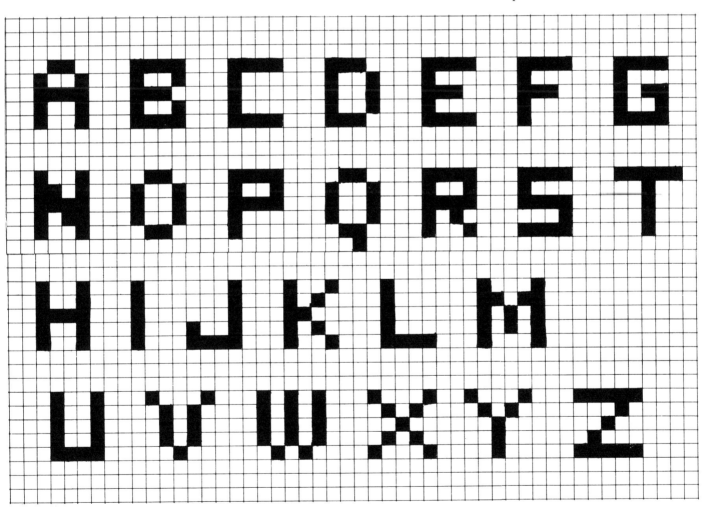

Alphabet 2

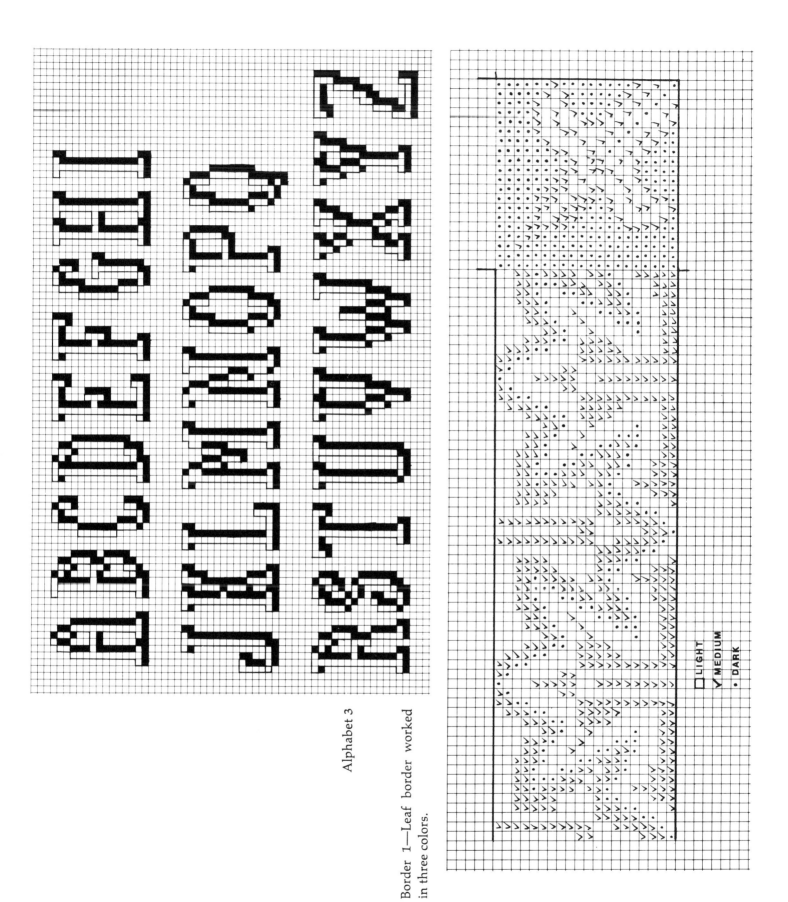

Alphabet 3

Border 1—Leaf border worked in three colors.

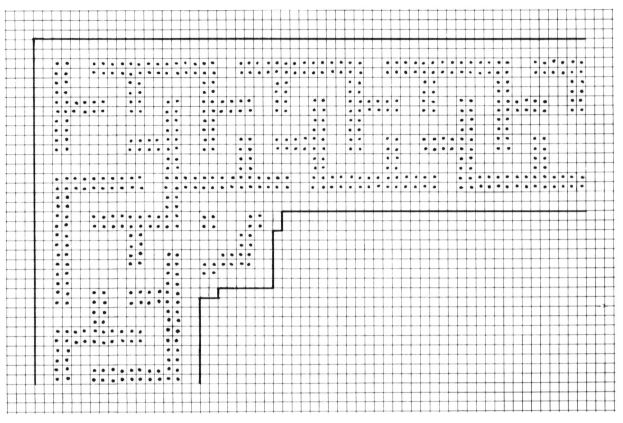

Border 2—Chinese border worked in two colors.

Border 3—Egg and dart in four colors—to be traced.

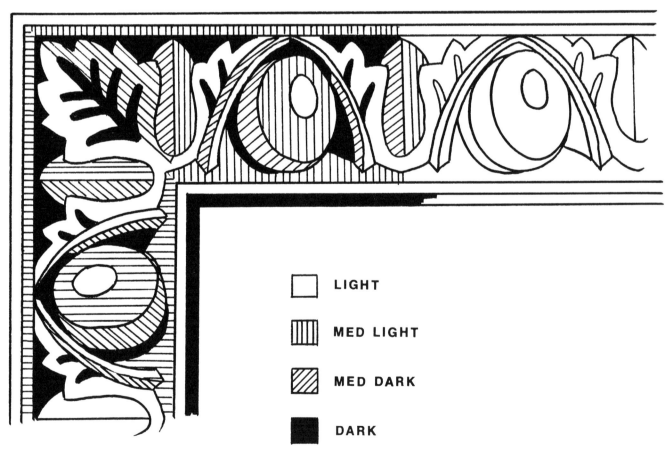

☐ LIGHT

▥ MED LIGHT

▨ MED DARK

■ DARK

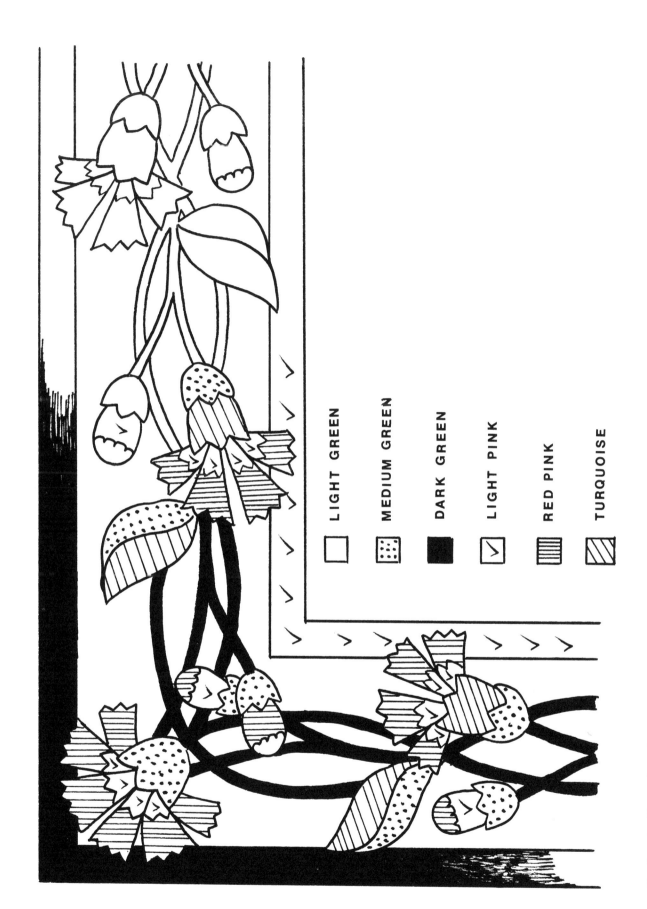

LIGHT GREEN

MEDIUM GREEN

DARK GREEN

LIGHT PINK

RED PINK

TURQUOISE

Border 4—Carnations in seven colors—to be traced.

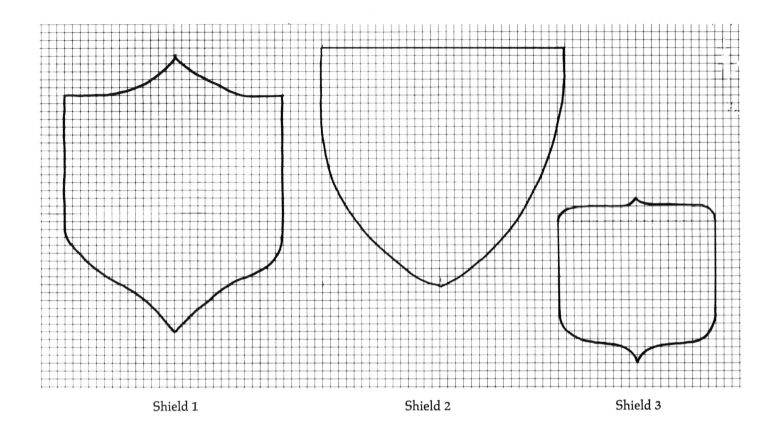

Shield 1   Shield 2   Shield 3

CHAPTER EIGHT

Tassels and Fringe

Cut a piece of cardboard an inch longer than you want your tassel to be when finished. Wind your yarn around the cardboard anywhere from twenty to forty times, depending on how bulky you want the tassel to be.

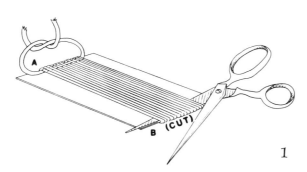

1

2   —— —TRIM 3

Steps in making a tassel.

Cut a piece of yarn about eight inches long, slip it under the yarn at the edge of your board (at point A in diagram) and tie a double knot. Keep these ends free of the tassel. Now cut through the yarn at point B in the diagram. Cut another piece of yarn about twenty-two inches long. Leaving an eight-inch length free at one end, wrap the yarn around the tassel, about one inch from the top, leaving an eight inch tail.

Thread the eight-inch tails into your needle and insert the needle into the wrapped yarn and bring the tails out the center top of the tassel where the two ends of the knotted yarn are.

You now have four ends of yarn coming out of the top of the tassel. These ends may now be threaded into your needle, one at a time. Go through your work from the right side with each strand where you want the tassel to hang, securing the end of each under worked stitches on the wrong side, using one backstitch to hold them securely.

If you want the top of the tassel to hang down a little away from the finished piece, plait the four threads for an inch or so before working them into the canvas.

FRINGE
As with the tassel, cut a piece of cardboard one inch longer than you want your fringe to be. Wrap the yarn around the board. Place a rubber band around the wrapped yarn and cut at one end.

Taking one strand, fold it in half and, with a crochet hook, pull the looped end through the wrong side of the canvas (1). Insert the two loose ends through the loop and tighten (2). Repeat this procedure, spacing strands evenly. For a thicker fringe, more than one strand may be used in each mesh.

For a knotted fringe, knot where indicated on the diagram below (3).

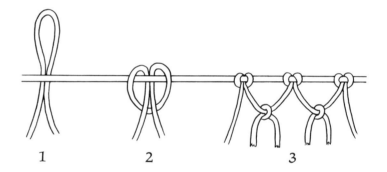

Tying and knotting fringe.

1   2   3

When fringing a prepared or finished edge, the knotting is done over the exposed thread of the finished edge. On rug canvas it is easiest to tie in the fringe with the use of a latch hook.

Latch Hook

When fringing a finished edge, work with the wrong side of the canvas facing up. Fold a piece of yarn in half over the shank of the hook (1). Insert the hook between the exposed thread and the first row of stitching, from *below*. Draw the two ends of the piece of yarn across the open latch (2). Letting go of the loose ends, draw hook toward you until the loose ends have been pulled through the looped yarn (3). Tighten knot by pulling ends firmly (4).

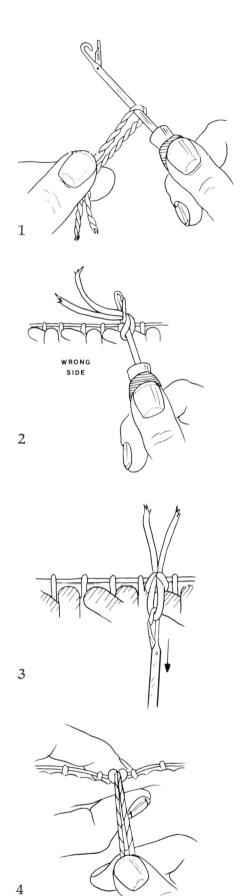

1

WRONG
SIDE

2

3

Adding fringe with the use of a latch hook.

4

Finishing Techniques

WELTING Many projects, notably pillows, are improved by the addition of a welting around the edges. You can buy commercially prepared weltings, if you can find the proper colors. Most often, I prefer making my own weltings, using the same fabric I have used for lining or backing a project.

Welting is always sewn between the needlepoint and the lining or backing material. To make your own, reserve a square of your backing fabric, or use a square of a contrasting colored fabric if you so desire, and find the true bias. This is done by folding the fabric so that the cut end (be sure it's cut perpendicular to the selvage) lies along the selvage. The fold so achieved is the true bias of the fabric.

Now cut along the fold and, measuring from this new edge, cut bias strips one and a half inches wide.

Now, on the sewing machine, sew the bias strips together, as diagramed, right sides together until you have the length you require.

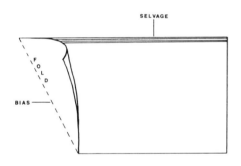

Finding the true bias.

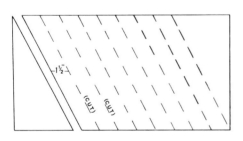

Cutting bias strips.

Sewing the bias strips together.

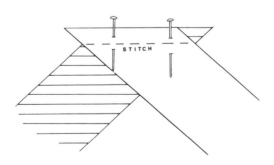

Buy welting cord at your notions shop. Place the cord in the center of your bias strip and, using the zipper foot on your sewing machine, stitch close to the cord (but not crowding), stretching your bias strip slightly as you stitch. Avoid stitching through the cord.

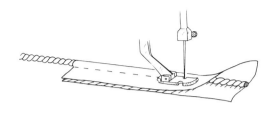

Sewing the cord into the bias strips.

Welting is attached after the needlepoint is blocked. Lay the work right side up and pin the welting to it with the corded edge of the welting toward the stitching and the cut edge of the welting toward the cut edge of the canvas. As you go around corners make snips in the raw edge of the welting to allow it to curve more easily. This applies to square corners as well as rounded. Make a sufficient number of snips in the raw edges of the welting to allow the cording to make the turn required easily.

To join two ends of welting, as you would for a pillow or anywhere else where the welting must be continuous, open the last inch of the seam of the welting at one end and cut off an inch of the cording. At this end of the welting, turn a half-inch of the fabric under, place it over and around the end of the welting that you began with, and pin it into place. Now baste the welting onto the needlework and, still with your zipper foot, stitch it on the machine, stitching over the seam that holds the cording in the welting.

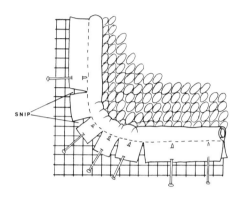

Pinning the welting to the blocked piece.

Note: When attaching continuous welting as for a pillow, I always start the welting in the center of the bottom edge, where the join is least likely to show.

Now take your backing piece and lay it face down on the needlepoint and welting (in other words, right sides together). Pin, baste and then, with the canvas side on top, machine stitch them together, again sewing over the seam line on the welting. Be sure to leave one side open for insertion of the pillow. Sew this last seam by hand.

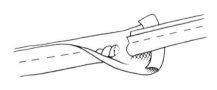

Joining two ends for a continuous welt.

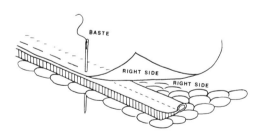

Adding the backing piece.

There are several ways to join two edges of worked needlepoint. The method you choose will depend on the nature of the project. For the projects in this book, the method to use is always indicated.

By Seaming

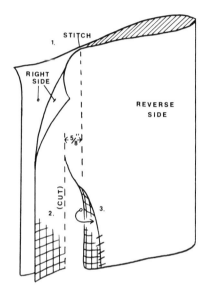

The simplest method is to make a seam the same way you would in joining two edges of fabric. This is serviceable only when it is not necessary to match a pattern or meshes.

Be sure you have at least three rows of extra stitched needlepoint as a seam allowance around the outside of the edges you are going to seam. And, of course, any kind of seaming should not be done until the work has been blocked.

With right sides facing each other, sew the two pieces of canvas together (1). Cut the excess unworked canvas away, leaving a seam allowance of about ⅝ inch (2). Be sure to glue the cut edges. When the glue is dry, press the seam open and whip the glued edges to the back of the needlepoint stitches (3).

By Whipping

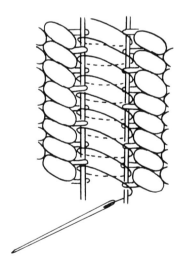

For a less noticeable join, two edges of canvas may be whipped together. This is a good method to use when joining two edges of a rectangle to make a cylinder as in the lamp base project or the wastebasket.

Cut away the excess unworked canvas, leaving a ⅝-inch seam allowance. Glue the cut edges. On each side to be joined, turn the unworked canvas under, leaving one unworked thread of canvas exposed. Matching the meshes to each other along each edge, whip them together with carpet thread. Now cover the thread with a vertical line of Continental stitches in the background color wool or, where patterns continue across the seam, keep changing the wool to the colors that will continue the pattern across the seam.

Some projects in the book will ask you to graft two pieces of canvas together. This is a virtually invisible join and is especially valuable when a project requires a canvas wider than those available.

First, cut away the selvages along the vertical edges of the two pieces of canvas to be grafted. Glue the edges. Lay one on top of the other so that five meshes overlap. Baste these carefully together. Now draw your design on this double piece of canvas as if it were one (1). Now take out your basting.

Needlepoint each of the two pieces of canvas separately, being sure to stop your work six or seven meshes before you arrive at the edges to be overlapped (2).

When you are ready to join the two pieces of canvas, lay the piece on which the design goes clear to the edge over the piece that has 5 meshes clear of design. Matching the two pieces mesh for mesh, whip them together with carpet thread, using a back stitch and covering one mesh at a time. When the two pieces of canvas are whipped together, continue to needlepoint across the overlapping canvas as if it were a single piece of canvas, using the same stitch you've used in the rest of the work (3).

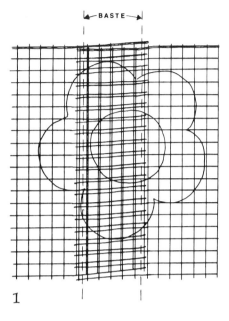

1

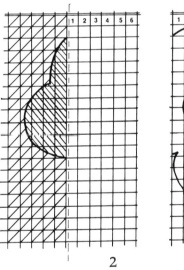 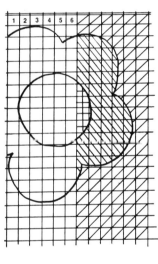

2

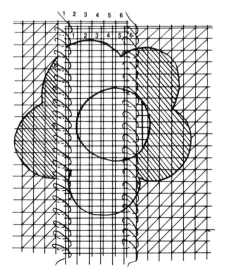

3

PART TWO

The Projects

PART TWO

The Projects

The Color Chart and Paterna Rug Yarns
Used in the Projects

Color Chart	Paterna Rug
5	437
6	442
7	441
8	440
15	958
32	739
37	365
53	020
63	445
66	395
67	005
70	050

Note: Paragon has a rug yarn developed especially for #5 canvas. Not made of wool, it is composed of 70 percent acrylic and 30 percent nylon. As the colors do not correspond to my color chart, the numbers are not included here. But if you are interested, you can look at Paragon's Charisma Multi-Purpose Speed Yarn chart in your needlepoint shop and select colors close to those in my color chart.

The Color Chart Numbers
with Corresponding Numbers of
Paterna 3-Ply Persian Yarns and
Paragon 3-Ply Persian Yarns

C.C. = Color Chart   Pat. = Paterna   Par. = Paragon

C.C.	Pat.	Par.	C.C.	Pat.	Par.	C.C.	Pat.	Par.
1	458	296	25	643	——	49	583	105
2	450	293	26	623	——	50	511	617
3	Y42	442	27	631	737	51	144	122
4	447	206	28	611	735	52	011	823
5	437	445	29	741	251	53	153	115
6	442	444	30	731	249	54	143	114
7	441	443	31	321	472	55	133	113
8	440	442	32	754	251	56	123	112
9	012	823	33	385	200	57	115	367
10	455	277	34	322	362	58	978	708
11	454	709	35	318	722	59	278	485
12	970	803	36	312	721	60	225	640
13	965	802	37	365	127	61	210	100
14	960	801	38	748	833	62	207	417
15	958	743	39	738	832	63	445	276
16	242	742	40	728	831	64	433	275
17	240	178	41	718	830	65	134	107
18	810	457	42	Y50	375	66	382	130
19	265	103	43	545	374	67	001	740
20	860	461	44	G64	713	68	184	385
21	260	102	45	575	146	69	180	382
22	831	194	46	527	438	70	050	285
23	828	258	47	563	646			
24	829	257	48	540	644			

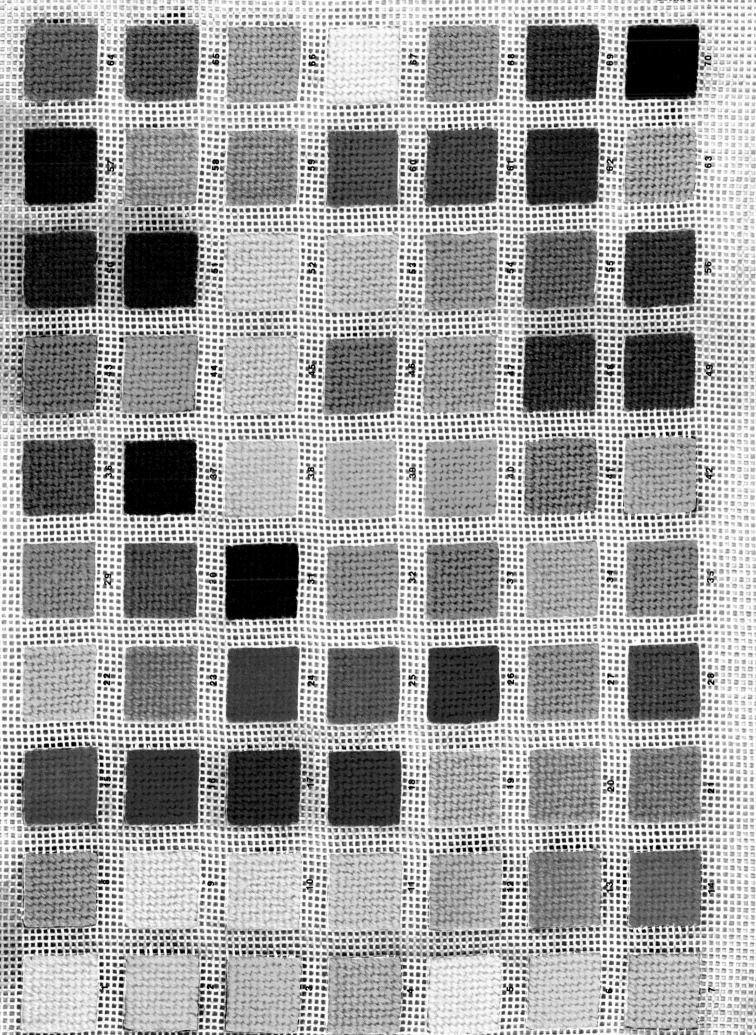
Color Chart

Top to bottom
Jewel Belt
Link Belt
Cummerbund and Bow Tie
Medallion Spectacle Case
Eye Chart Spectacle Case

Left to right,
on the Circular Table Cover
Ice Bucket
Tassel Basket
Shell Tiles

Lamp Base and Shade

Clockwise from the top,
on the "Tile" Rug
Gift Box Pillow
Repeat Pattern Pillow
Lady's Vest
Chinese Pillow

HE NEVER MAKES ANY PROGRESS UNTIL HE STICKS HIS NECK OUT REMEMBER THE TURTLE

Turtle Plaque
Tiffany Tile

Top to bottom
Chair Seat
Backgammon Board
Dice Box

Two "Tile" Rugs

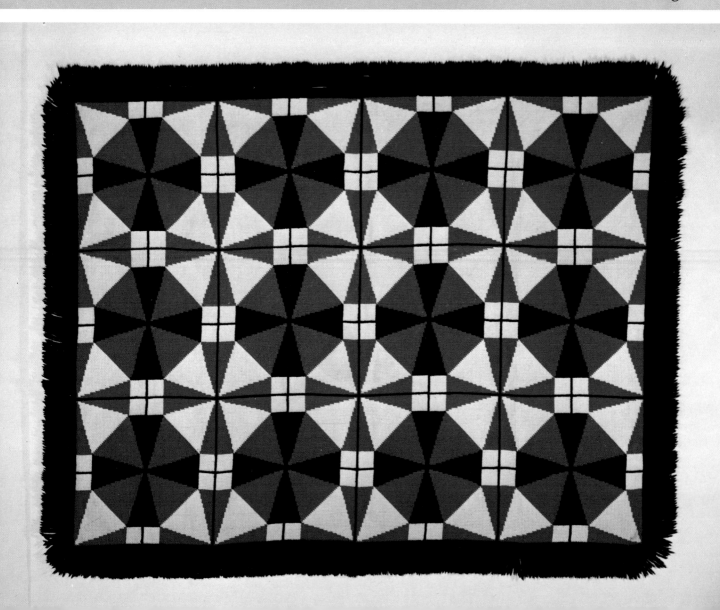

PROJECT 1

Eye Chart Spectacle Case

I don't suggest this eye chart for an examination, but at least you can use it to test your specs for cleanliness.

I have worked the whole case, both design and background, on a #16 mono canvas as I preferred the more delicate look of the small stitches in the background as well as the design. However, if you wish, you may use an 8/16 penelope

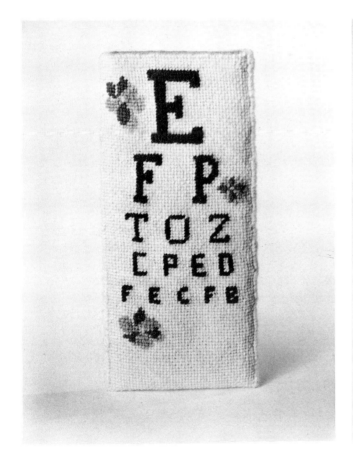
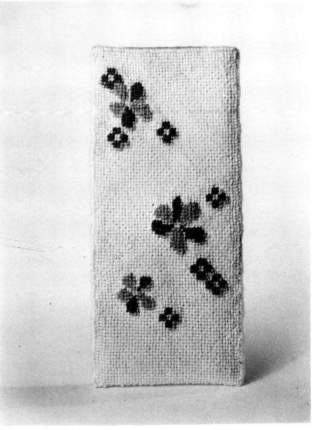

canvas, working the design sixteen stitches to the inch and the background eight stitches to the inch.

CANVAS For #16 mono—one piece 58 meshes wide by 14½ inches long.
For 8/16 penelope canvas—one piece 31 double meshes wide by 14½ inches long.

WOOL Three-ply Persian. For #16 mono canvas use two plies for each thread for the design but only one ply for each thread for the background.
For 8/16 penelope use two plies for each thread for the design and the full three plies for each thread for the background.

OUNCES	COLORS ILLUSTRATED
½	67
¼	70
⅛	25
¼	27
⅛	2
⅛	26

PREPARATION *For mono canvas:* Glue cut edges. Hem each of the four sides for a finished edge (p. 36) turning hems back between the fourth and fifth meshes on each side.
For penelope canvas: Glue cut edges. Hem each side for a finished edge, turning each hem back on the third double mesh.

STITCHING Use the Basketweave stitch wherever possible.

BLOCKING Block to your paper pattern in the conventional way for a finished edge (p. 43), being sure to place your pins between the finished work and the exposed mesh, *not* into the wool stitches. Treat with rabbit-skin glue.

Braid stitch the top and bottom (p. 32), using one ply of yarn
in your needle.

Obtain a piece of felt, preferably the same color as one of
the colors in the flowers. Cut a piece the same width as your
finished piece and one inch longer than your finished piece.
Turn back a half-inch at top and bottom and hem. Fold the
length in half and sew a quarter-inch seam on each side. Cut
away one eighth of an inch from these side seams.

Whip one side of the top of the felt envelope to the Braid
stitching at the front top of your needlework.

Fold your needlework in half lengthwise, so that the
front top and the back top are even.

Braid stitch the sides together, using one ply of yarn for
each thread.

Now whip the back top of the felt envelope to the back
top braid stitching.

Spray lightly several times with Scotchgard.

PROJECT 2

Turtle Plaque

"Remember the Turtle. He never makes any progress until he sticks his neck out." Not a bad reminder to yourself, or a not-so-gentle hint to a good friend.

CANVAS   #10 mono. A piece approximately 18 by 22 inches.

WOOL   Three-ply Persian. Use full three plies for each thread.

OUNCES	COLORS ILLUSTRATED	ALTERNATES	
		YELLOW	PINK
⅛	12	1	22
⅛	14	2	23
1	16	4	26
¼	15	3	25
1	43	64	18
¼	42	63	24
4¼	50	44	67

PREPARATION

Apply masking tape to all cut edges.

In this project, the turtle is traced onto the canvas and the letters are worked from a graph. Stitch the letters first, then trace the turtle in the center of the rectangle formed by the letters.

STITCHING

Use the Basketweave stitch wherever possible. The border may be stitched with the Basketweave stitch, as in the illustration, or you may want to add some texture to it by using the Double Cross stitch. Start working at the center of the top line of the graph, leaving 2½ inches of unworked canvas above the letters. Remember that one square on the graph represents one stitch. (See page 38.)

BLOCKING   Block in the conventional way, face down, to your paper pattern, and treat with rabbit-skin glue.

FINISHING   Cut a piece of plywood to the exact size of the blocked needlepoint. Turn the unworked canvas over the plywood and staple to the back. Insert in a 14-by-18-inch frame.

     If you have it framed professionally, tell your framer to mount the needlepoint on board before framing.

PROJECT 3

Jewel Belt

The belt illustrated simulates turquoises set into a gold chain with gold studs along the edges. The "jewels" can be changed to rubies, sapphires or topaz, by using the alternate colors given below.

For a man, change the gold chain and studs to silver, the background to dark brown, use a large silver western buckle and you'll have a stunning western-style belt.

Note: The motifs in this design may be used for border motifs in other projects.

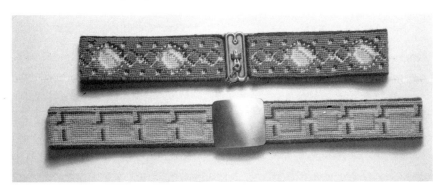

CANVAS #10 mono canvas.
Start with a piece of canvas five inches wide. The length is determined by the waist measurement plus six inches, minus the width of the buckle to be used. For example, if the waist is thirty inches, six inches added would bring the measurement to thirty-six inches. If you are going to use a buckle three inches wide, subtract three inches from the thirty-six, making the total length of canvas required thirty-three inches.

WOOL Three-ply Persian, use full three plies for each thread.

| | | | ALTERNATES | | |
OUNCES	COLORS ILLUSTRATED	SAPPHIRE	RUBY	TOPAZ	WESTERN
1/8	67	67	67	67	67
1/8	10	10	38	38	52
1/8	4	4	40	40	68
1/8	64	64	41	41	69
1/8	38	34	15	12	38
1/8	40	35	16	13	40
1/8	41	36	17	60	41
1/8	31	69	48	70	51
1	28	68	43	51	65

PREPARATION Bind canvas with masking tape. Mark the middle of the canvas.
A repeat pattern is given to accommodate any length required.

STITCHING Use the Continental stitch for design and the Basketweave stitch for background.
I found it easiest to start at the center top of the canvas, stitching the "studs" first. Work to the right until you've worked one-half of your total waist measurement, minus buckle allowance. Then work the other half to the left. Next work the studs on the bottom of the belt. These will serve as handy reference points when working the "jewels" and the "chains." Try to end with some "chain" on each end to join to the buckle.

Block in the conventional manner (pp. 43–45), and treat with rabbit-skin glue.

Leave five meshes of unworked canvas around entire belt. Cut off excess and glue raw edges. Turn unworked canvas to the back of the work and, leaving two meshes exposed on all sides, stitch to back of work. Braid stitch (p. 32) entire perimeter with your darkest shade of wool.

Use two-inch grosgrain ribbon or blanket binding for lining. Working from the center out, whip the lining to the Braid stitches, inserting each buckle half between lining and belt before whipping the lining to the ends. I find that two-part buckles are much the most serviceable for needlepoint belts.

PROJECT 4

Link Belt

This two-inch belt may, obviously, be worn by either men or women. No alternate colors are given for the links, as I feel they should simulate gold. However, the background may be changed to any medium shade you wish. Remember, however, that when you change the color of the background, you must change the color of the shadows the "links" cast on the background. In the illustrated belt the background is a medium gray, the shadows the "links" cast on the background are done in a charcoal gray. If, then, you decide on a blue background, you will have to select a medium shade of blue and a dark shade, like a navy, for the shadows (the lines that are stitched in charcoal on the illustrated belt).

As with the belt in project 3, this is worked on a #10 mono canvas. All the instructions for project 3 apply to this project, with the exception of the colors used and the amounts of each color.

WOOL Three-ply Persian. Use full three-ply for each thread.

OUNCES	COLORS ILLUSTRATED
¾	68
½	69
¾	4
¼	64

PROJECT 5

Chinese Pillow

A crisp, smart accent, this design works extremely well for other projects as well as the 14-inch pillow illustrated.

It's stunning when used for chair backs or seats. It will also make a handsome ottoman.

The design is easily enlarged, either by adding more background or enlarging the design itself. To enlarge the design, just be sure to add as many stitches to every vertical "bar" of the design as you do to every horizontal "bar."

#10 mono. One-half yard of 24-inch canvas.   *CANVAS*

WOOL   Three-ply Persian. Use full three plies for each thread.

| | | ALTERNATES | | |
OUNCES	COLORS ILLUSTRATED	GOLD	RED	BLUE
1	48	64	15	29
1	70	50	17	36
3	53	53	53	53

PREPARATION   Start with a piece of canvas eighteen inches square. Bind edges with masking tape.

Find the center of your canvas and, referring to the graph provided, designate the center square of the design with indelible marker.

STITCHING   Using the Basketweave stitch, stitch the center square of the design. Then stitch each of the four corner motifs.

Extend the background eleven rows on each side of the design for a 14-inch pillow. This gives you an allowance of three rows of stitches to be taken into the seams when the backing is applied.

BLOCKING   Block to your 18-inch paper pattern, making sure the sides are absolutely perpendicular to the top and bottom. Be sure to treat with rabbit-skin glue.

FINISHING   Leaving one-half inch of unworked canvas on all four sides, cut off the excess and glue all cut edges with Sobo.

Finish with welting, referring to instructions in chapter 9.

Repeat Pattern for Pillow or Upholstery

This pattern has been designed so that it may be used for a pillow, as illustrated, or for upholstered pieces such as piano benches, love seats, chair seats and backs, etc. It will also make a beautiful fireplace screen or folding screen. In other words, it can be used to cover as large or small an area as is required.

The pattern provided will match perfectly and make a continuous pattern when repeated horizontally or vertically.

The pattern is sixteen inches square. Should you need, for example, a piece large enough to upholster a piano bench twenty inches by thirty-six inches, use the pattern, or parts of it, nine times, as in the diagram below. The pattern is indicated by dotted lines.

As the color balance is so complex and will complement

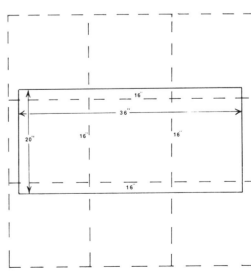

practically any color scheme, alternate colors are not given. But the background color, illustrated in a light yellow, may be changed to white, light blue, light pink, or almost any other pastel shade.

CANVAS #14 mono. ⅔ yard, 40 inches wide, will give you sufficient canvas for two 16-inch pillows or enough for most benches, including piano benches.

WOOL (for a 16-inch Pillow)
Three-ply Persian. Use only two plies in each thread.

OUNCES	COLOR	OUNCES	COLOR
½	33	¼	24
½	39	½	4
½	43	½	44
¼	67	½	20
3¼	10	½	18
½	3	½	15
¼	26	¼	27
¼	42	¼	28
¾	64	½	46
¼	58	¼	31
¼	25		

PREPARATION If making a pillow, start with a piece of canvas twenty inches by twenty inches. Bind canvas with masking tape. Lay pattern under canvas and trace (p. 36), leaving two inches of blank canvas on each side of the pattern.

If using the pattern as a repeat for an item wider than the canvas, use the method for adding width described under "Grafting" in chapter 9.

STITCHING Use the Continental stitch for the more complex parts of the design, but use the Basketweave stitch for larger areas and all of the background. When using the design for a pillow, add three extra rows of stitches on all four sides to be sewn into seams.

Block, right side down, as described in chapter 6.   *BLOCKING*

Finish either as a knife-edged pillow, following directions in   *FINISHING*
chapter 9, or as a boxed pillow, as in Project 7. I used light   *FOR A PILLOW*
acid-green suede for backing the illustrated model.

Fourteen-Inch Gift Box Pillow

You can be pretty sure that the person who has everything doesn't have one of these.

The illustrated pillow was done entirely in needlepoint—top, sides and back. If you feel less ambitious, do only the top and sides in needlepoint and the back in fabric.

Use any message you wish on the "gift card" but be sure to work it out on the graph pattern before you stitch it. The letters in Alphabet 1 best fit the space provided.

In case you're curious, the "Tec" on the illustrated pillow is my nickname—which, I'm sure, you, too, would prefer were your name Morton. "Isobel" is one of the long-suffering sisters I often press into service with the needle.

#10 mono canvas. CANVAS

For top and sides only: One piece 15 inches square
One piece 3½ inches by 58 inches

For top, sides and back: Two pieces 15 inches square
One piece 3½ inches by 58 inches.

Note: As this pillow is worked on pieces with finished edges, it is best to count threads, rather than using a ruler. The top and bottom squares require 143 threads to be worked plus four on each side to turn back and hem. So your pieces should count 151 threads by 151 threads. The piece for the sides should have 24 threads to be worked plus 4 on top and 4 on bottom to turn back and hem. So your piece should be 32 threads wide. This piece requires 572 threads for length plus an inch to turn under on each end, or a total of 592 threads. You will find it easier to keep track when counting threads, to make a faint pencil mark after every tenth thread. This piece may be grafted together from shorter pieces if you want to be more economical (see "Grafting" in chapter 9).

Three-ply Persian—use full three plies in each thread. WOOL

OUNCES	COLORS ILLUSTRATED	PINK
1¾	34	23
¼	35	24
½	36	18
¼	31	62
¼	33	20
¼	30	26
¼	39	39
¼	43	43
4½	29	25
5½	52	22
⅛	67	67

Cut out canvas as required and glue all cut edges. PREPARATION

Hem all sides for finished edges, in each instance turning back four threads—except for the two ends of the long piece, in which case you turn back ten threads.

Note: If you are doing the back in fabric, do not hem one side of the long piece. These extra four threads will be used as seam allowance when joined to the fabric.

Following the graph, with your indelible marker (light blue) mark the width of the stripes. This will make it easier for you to do the rest of your counting. Count carefully—not all stripes are the same width. The blue stripes cover 21 threads and the off-white stripes cover 19 threads—*except* for the last two stripes on the right of the pillow. The last off-white covers 20 threads, and the last blue covers 22 threads.

STITCHING   I think you will find it easiest to work the "ribbons" and "bow" first. Work the entire pillow, wherever possible, with the Basketweave stitch.

If you are going to do the back of the pillow in fabric, work three extra rows of stitches on the bottom edge of the long boxing piece to be worked into the seam when you add the fabric.

If you like, you may overcast the stitches of the "string" and the edges of the "gift card" with a double strand of metallic silver thread as I did on the illustrated pillow.

BLOCKING   The sweater blocker, described under "Blocking" in project 18 is very useful for this project. You just arrange your pins into a fourteen-inch square and slip the exposed threads along the edges over these pins. Steam and apply rabbit-skin glue. If you don't have the sweater blocker, block in the conventional way, putting your rustproof pins between the exposed threads and the finished work—*not* into the finished stitches. Your long boxing piece may be blocked on the sweater blocker, a third at a time, or blocked in the conventional way.

ASSEMBLING   Starting at the lower right-hand corner, whip the boxing piece to the top, matching stitch for stitch. Now Braid stitch over the whipping stitches, changing colors to match the "stripes" and "shadows" that you are joining together. When you have joined the side to the top all the way around and come to the lower right-hand corner again, Braid stitch the two ends of the boxing piece together.

If you have worked the back in needlepoint whip it to the boxing piece—again being sure to match stitches. *Be sure* to insert your pillow form in the casing before you stitch the last side. Braid stitch over the whipping stitches, being sure to match stitches and colors. After you have completed three sides, insert your pillow form, whipstitch and Braid stitch the last side.

If you are using fabric for the back, turn the work inside out. Slit the canvas seam allowances in the corners up to the stitching. Cut a piece of fabric 15¼ inches square. Baste three sides to the boxing piece so that your machine stitching will take three rows of wool stitches into the seam. Sew these three sides on the sewing machine. Turn the work right side out, insert your pillow and whip the fourth side together by hand.

PROJECT 8

Ice Bucket

The needlepoint in this project is designed to be inserted in a plastic ice bucket especially designed for needlepoint. These buckets are available at most needlepoint shops, but if you have difficulty in obtaining one you may write directly to the distributor:

> Benay Venuta Designs
> 50 East 79th Street
> New York, N.Y. 10021

The outside measurements of the bucket are eight inches high with a circumference of 23½ inches. It has double walls between which the needlepoint is inserted so that it is protected from any dampness.

Cut a piece 28 inches wide by 12 inches long.

Three-ply Persian. Use a single ply to work the design, three   *WOOL*
plies for the background.

As the fruits are done in their natural colors, no alternates
are given.

OUNCES	COLORS ILLUSTRATED
⅛	42
⅛	1
⅛	10
¼	36
⅛	41
⅛	64
⅛	39
⅛	18
⅛	15
⅛	2
⅛	46
⅛	43
⅛	13
¼	3
1	67

Bind canvas with masking tape. Center design on canvas and   *PREPARATION*
trace.

STITCHING Everything except the white background is stitched in small stitches, sixteen stitches to the inch. The white background is stitched in large stitches, eight stitches to the inch. For the small stitches use one ply of the three-ply thread. For the background use a full three-ply thread.

BLOCKING Block, in the conventional manner, to a 12-by-28-inch rectangle.

FINISHING Leave five meshes of unworked canvas around the entire design. Cut away excess and glue edges. Turn back hems, leaving a double mesh on each side for Braid stitching. Whip hems down to back of stitches. Braid stitch long edges in white.

Now, line the piece, preferably with a light-weight white synthetic fabric. Whip lining to the top and sides, but only line to within one-half inch of the bottom, so the piece won't be too bulky to fit into the slot at the bottom of the plastic bucket.

After the piece is lined, butt the two ends and braid stitch them together. Insert in the ice bucket.

Tassel Basket

Use it as a wastebasket, a basket for magazines or as a vase for a dried arrangement.

The graph provided is for a piece of needlepoint large enough to cover a basket twelve inches tall by twenty-eight inches in circumference. For a larger basket, additional height can be added by adding more background color below the

design to a longer piece of canvas. To achieve a greater circumference, more area can be covered by leaving more space between the "tassels." There are ten spaces between "tassels" when the work is sewed together. As the design is worked on a #10 canvas, there are 10 stitches to the inch. If, for example, you need an additional inch for the circumference, you will need one additional vertical row of background in each space between the "tassels." For an additional two inches, you will need two extra vertical rows of stitches between "tassels."

Be sure to use either a round or oval basket, the top and bottom of which have the same measurements. In other words, do not use a tapered basket.

CANVAS #10 mono canvas.

Measure the height and circumference of the basket you are going to cover and cut a piece of canvas four inches wider than the circumference and four inches longer than the height of the basket. Place the design so that you have two inches of unworked canvas on all four sides.

WOOL Three-ply Persian. Use the full three plies in each thread.

OUNCES	COLORS ILLUSTRATED	YELLOW
½	24	8
¼	18	64
2	27	12
¼	25	3
¼	28	14
¼	67	67
½	23	7
6	22	6

PREPARATION Prepare top of canvas for a finished edge. Bind the other edges with masking tape.

STITCHING Stitch all of the "tassels." Stitch background with Basketweave stitch. As everyone's work varies in tightness, work background to about one inch from the bottom before you determine where your bottom edge will come. Keep trying the work against the basket. When your work has reached the point within one inch of your bottom edge, you should be able to determine at which mesh the background must stop. Before proceeding, prepare the bottom for a finished edge. Complete the background.

BLOCKING

Block in the conventional way for a piece of work with a finished edge. The rectangle to which you block should measure vertically the same as the vertical measurement of your basket. The horizontal measurement should be the same as the measurement of the piece of canvas you started with.

FINISHING

After blocking, be sure the two vertical worked edges meet when wrapped around your basket. If you are short, add as many rows of stitches to each edge as you need. Leave five meshes of unworked canvas, cut off excess and glue edges. Turn back the two hems and stitch down to the back of the work, leaving two meshes exposed for the Braid stitch. Work Braid stitch in background color along top and bottom and both edges that are to be joined. With wrong side of canvas facing you, butt the two edges to be joined and whip together with matching cotton thread. Turn work right side out and slip the tube over the basket.

A further trim may be added, as in the illustrated basket, by making a braid (plaiting) of some or all of the colors of wools you've used. Secure each end of the braid with cotton thread. Use Sobo glue and glue the braid to the top of the needlepoint, being sure the join is placed at the back seam.

Medallion Spectacle Case

A good way of presenting a medal—even if it's only for wearing glasses. If my friends are any criteria, most men would welcome this personalized case.

The one illustrated is worked in smart colors that will go well with most masculine attire. However, alternate colors are suggested for the "ribbon," background and shadow.

#14 mono. One piece 52 meshes wide by 14½ inches long. *CANVAS*

Three-ply Persian. Use two plies for each thread. *WOOL*

| | | ALTERNATES | | |
OUNCES	COLORS ILLUSTRATED	GRAY	BLUE	MAROON
¼	43	30	43	28
¼	42	15	3	27
¾	50	68	36	17
¼	67	67	67	52
⅛	4	4	4	4
¼	51	69	37	51
⅛	10	10	10	10
⅛	64	64	64	64

Note: For the gold stripes in the "ribbon" of the illustrated case, use one ply of #4 and one ply of #64.

All steps for preparation are the same as those given for project 1 (Eye Chart Spectacle Case) with one addition. It is necessary for you to enter the initials you want to use in the medallion on the graph for this project. Use the letters from Alphabet 3 on the alphabet graph. On the graph for this project, the space on the "medallion" for initials is 26 stitches wide by 14 stitches high. Determine from the alphabet graph how many stitches each letter you require takes up and divide the space accordingly. *PREPARATION*

All instructions for blocking and finishing are the same as they are for Project 1 (Eye Chart Spectacle Case) with the following exception. All Braid stitching should be done in the background color with two plies of yarn in your needle. *BLOCKING AND FINISHING*

PROJECT 11

Chair Seat

This design will adapt to almost any size chair seat. No alternate colors are given, as the design works best in the shades of gold in the illustrated model. However, you may choose any color for the background that complements your decor. Use a darker shade of your background color for the shadow the design casts on the background.

I suggest you have your upholsterer give you a paper pattern, or template, of exactly the size piece of upholstery he will need to cover your chair seat.

#10 mono. Enough to accommodate your template with a   CANVAS
margin of two inches on all sides.

Three-ply Persian. Use the full three plies for each thread.   WOOL

OUNCES	COLORS ILLUSTRATED
2	5
2	63
2	65
2	49

On the illustrated chair seat #15 was used for the background and #17 for the shadows the design throws onto the background. You will need about 1½ ounces of background shadow color. The amount of wool for your background depends on the size of your chair seat. I would surmise that you will need at least six ounces.

Stitch the design first, using the Basketweave stitch wherever   STITCHING
possible, the Continental stitch where the design is too intricate for Basketweave. Then stitch the shadow the design casts. Next, using the Basketweave stitch, stitch the background up to the template outline.

Block, face down, to the paper pattern of your full canvas   BLOCKING
rectangle (not to the outline of the template). Treat with rabbit-skin glue.

Do not cut away excess canvas. Turn the whole piece over to   FINISHING
your upholsterer and leave it to him to cut away whatever he has to.

PROJECT 12

Backgammon Board

I believe that this is handsome enough to hang on the wall when not in use. Or you may have it mounted on the top of a game table. Many hours of work are required, but they are justified by the end result.

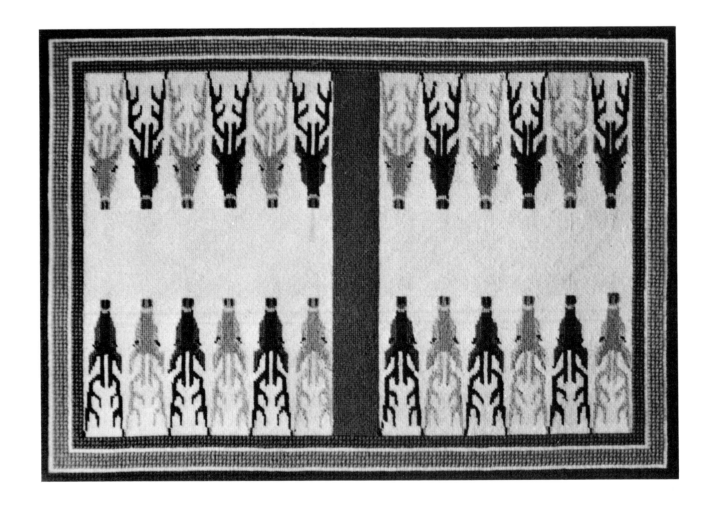

#12 mono. One piece 34 inches by 26 inches.   *CANVAS*

Three-ply Persian. Use only two plies for each thread.   *WOOL*

OUNCES	COLORS ILLUSTRATED
5	67
⅛	70
½	53
⅛	54
2	56
3	55
2	57

Apply masking tape to all four edges of your canvas. Be sure   *PREPARATION*
to make a paper pattern of your piece of canvas, marking cen-
ters on all four sides of both the canvas and the paper pattern.
Trace the design onto the canvas with indelible marker.

Stitch the reindeer first, wherever possible in Basketweave   *STITCHING*
stitch. Where design is too intricate for Basketweave, use Continental stitch. Then stitch the center divider and the white
background, using the Basketweave stitch.

The border is composed of rows of Double Cross stitch, sepa-   *BORDER*
rated by rows of Continental stitch. For the Double Cross
stitches, use two plies for each thread, the same as you have
for the rest of the canvas.

    1. The innermost border is made up of three rows of
Double Cross stitch worked in color #56.
    2. Next work two rows of Continental stitch in color
#67 (white).
    3. Next work four rows of Double Cross stitch in color
#55.
    4. Next work two rows of Continental stitch in color
#67 (white).
    5. Next work three rows of Double Cross stitch in color
#57. This completes the outer border.

BLOCKING   Block face down on your paper pattern in the usual way. Steam thoroughly. Treat with rabbit-skin glue.

FINISHING   If you are going to mount the work on a tabletop, I suggest that you get an upholsterer to do the work.

If you wish the board to be portable or to hang on the wall, cut a piece of plywood to the exact size of the edge of the outer border. Work two rows of Continental stitch in color #57 next to the outer border to cover the thickness of the plywood.

Lay the work on the plywood, pull the unworked canvas neatly to the back and lace the edges or secure with staples. When using the lacing method, use heavy carpet thread. Lace from top to bottom and from side to side, taking up at least three meshes every time the needle goes through the canvas. Cut a piece of thin foam rubber (not more than one-quarter inch thick) to the size of the plywood. Cover one side of the foam rubber with brown felt, being sure to cover the edges of the rubber by bringing an inch of the felt around the edges to the wrong side of the rubber. Glue the felt to the foam rubber. Glue the uncovered side of the foam rubber to the back of the backgammon board.

You will notice in the photograph that I covered the dice box in needlepoint. Merely prepare a piece of canvas high

enough to cover the height of the box plus sufficient extra meshes for a finished edge top and bottom. The length should be about an inch and a half longer than the circumference. I started at the top with two rows of Double Cross stitch in color #57, followed by a single row of Continental stitch in white (#67). Next, three rows of Double Cross stitch in #55, followed by one row of Continental stitch in #67. Next, two rows of Double Cross stitch in #56. Follow this with two rows of Continental stitch in #67. Then I mirrored what I had done above, starting with two rows of Double Cross stitch in #56.

To block, turn back the excess canvas on each end to the back of the work and sew it down, leaving two meshes exposed.

Butt the two ends and Braid stitch together. Now Braid stitch the top and bottom circumferences and slip the cover over box.

If your box is taller than the 34 meshes worked on mine, adjust by making the center white strip wider.

If your box is shorter, remove one row of Double Cross stitch from each band of #55.

Lamp Base

This has turned out to be one of my favorite projects.

Before starting this project, go to any custom lamp maker and get from him a round wooden post 4½ inches in diameter (14½ inch circumference) and 17 inches tall, drilled through the center for wiring.

As the design is based on Greek motifs, I have used the characteristic colors of black, white and terra-cotta. You may substitute any other color for the terra-cotta if it does not complement your decor.

When a shade is added, the overall height of this lamp is 37 inches. If you require a smaller lamp, reduce the circumference by one or two motifs and the height two or more bands.

If you have difficulty securing the parts for this project, write to me in care of the publisher and I will refer you to a source that will send you everything you need to assemble it.

Note: Any band of this design may be used as a border on other projects. To accommodate this I have given extra corner motifs on the graph in case you want to use the bands as borders. I want to make it clear, however, that the corner motifs are *not* used in this lamp project.

Also note that a combination of these bands may be used for straps on a luggage rack. Use two or three bands together on strips of canvas with finished edges. The finished width of the bands should be 2 or 2½ inches.

CANVAS   #12 mono. Cut a piece 22 inches wide by 25 inches long.

Three-ply Persian. Use only two plies in each thread.

		ALTERNATES	
OUNCES	COLORS ILLUSTRATED	BLUE	GREEN
2	70	70	70
3½	67	67	67
2	60	30	44

Bind the edges of your canvas with masking tape.   *PREPARATION*

Find the center of the width and, with a light indelible marker, draw a line from top to bottom indicating the center.

From the center, count off 90 threads to the right and draw another vertical line. Now count off 90 stitches to the left and draw a vertical line. You have now established the width of the area to be worked.

Leaving two inches of unworked canvas at the top, refer to the graph for this project and start drawing in horizontal lines, indicating the width of each stripe and motif area. This will make it easier for you to count when you are stitching.

Note that only half of the design, both horizontally and vertically, is graphed. For the width, merely continue to work the design across the ungraphed half as you did the charted half. The lower part of the lamp base is a *mirrored* repetition of the top half.

Special Note: The "bird and tree" border is at the center of the base of the lamp and is only used *once*. In other words, when you have completed the "bird and tree" border, below that you will begin to repeat borders, starting with the Greek key.

Remember to use only two plies of wool in your needle. Stitch   *STITCHING*
as much as you can with the Basketweave stitch, filling in the rest with Continental.

Block by the conventional method, being sure to treat the back   *BLOCKING*
of the work with rabbit-skin glue.

Leaving five meshes of unworked canvas along every edge,   *FINISHING*
cut off the excess, first making sure that the worked canvas

completely covers the circumference of the post and the length top to bottom. Glue the cut edges. Sew hems down to the back of the work, leaving two meshes exposed for Braid stitch. Braid stitch the top and bottom in black and the two sides in white.

Wrap the finished work around the wooden post and whip the two rows of Braid stitching together with white cotton thread.

Note: If your finished work turns out to be slightly larger than the circumference of your wooden post, you may glue a piece of felt onto the post to take up the slack.

When you have applied the finished work to the post, take it back to your custom lamp man who will wire the lamp and put a base and a cap on the post. (I suggest these be done in black.) He will also provide a harp and the finial (also black) for the shade.

It is not necessary to have a shade custom-made. You can get a ready-made one in any department store. A parchment or linen shade is most fitting for this base. I suggest a drum shade 17 inches deep with a diameter of 17 inches at the bottom and 16 inches at the top.

To customize a shade yourself, see the next project.

PROJECT 14

Lamp Shade

This shade was especially developed to complement the lamp base in project 13.

The motif and edgings are applied to a ready-made shade, available in most department stores.

It is important that the shade be translucent, as the design is worked to be silhouetted when the lamp is turned on. The shade I used is made of linen stretched over translucent vinyl.

The shade is drum-shaped and measures 17 inches in depth with a bottom diameter of 17 inches and a top diameter of 16 inches.

#12 mono. You will need a piece approximately 12 inches by 7 inches.

CANVAS

Three-ply Persian. Use only two plies for work.

WOOL

| | | ALTERNATES | |
OUNCES	COLORS ILLUSTRATED	BLUE	GREEN
¾	70	70	70
⅛	60	30	44

Cut out a piece of canvas exactly 130 threads wide by 78 threads high. Glue cut edges and allow them to dry.

Turn back hems on each side between the third and fourth threads. Whip them down with white thread for a

PREPARATION

finished edge. Make a pattern of the hemmed piece for block-ing purposes.

STITCHING   As the motifs are worked for a silhouette effect when the lamp is lighted, great care must be taken not to cross areas on the back with yarn where the canvas is to be left exposed. Only the three motifs of the design and the border are stitched. The rest of the canvas is left unworked.

BLOCKING   Block, in the conventional way for a finished-edge piece, to your paper pattern. Be sure to put your pins between the worked stitches and the exposed threads, *not* into the worked stitches.

FINISHING   Work a Braid stitch in the terra-cotta wool around all four sides.

On the center front of the shade (opposite the side with the seam), make light pencil marks to indicate where the plaque is to be placed—equidistant from the top and bottom of the shade.

Carefully apply a fine line of Sobo glue to the back side of the Braid-stitch edging and glue the plaque to the shade.

The shade will be doubly enhanced by putting ribbon borders around the top and bottom circumferences.

You may buy ½-inch ribbon in black, white and terra-cotta and, with Sobo glue, apply a band of each to the top and to the bottom. Or you may be as fortunate as I was and find a one-inch ribbon that has black, white and terra-cotta stripes woven into it.

PROJECT 15

Lady's Vest

This is an accessory that can make a stunning costume out of any basic garment. Wear it with a shirt and slacks or over an evening dress. It can be worn over white, yellow, turquoise, gold, orange or pink.

Don't be intimidated by the design—it's much easier than it looks. It is worked on a #10 canvas with a design that is slightly more detailed than is adaptable to that large a mesh so that the design will have a slightly irregular "peasanty"

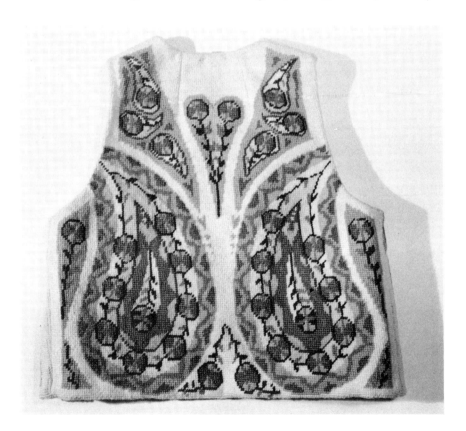

look. Of course, if you want the design to look "finer" you may use a 10/20 penelope canvas, working parts of the design in petit point and others in gros point. I strongly recommend, however, that you do it all in gros point for a marvelous effect.

The pattern provided is size 10. If you require a smaller or larger size, the pattern closest to the one provided is Simplicity #8288. The design can be easily adapted to smaller and larger sizes of that pattern.

CANVAS   #10 mono canvas.

Three pieces are required—left front, right front, and back. Cut two pieces 18 inches wide by 26 inches long for left front and right front. Cut one piece 26 inches by 26 inches for the back. These dimensions should be sufficient for sizes from 8 to 12. Add an extra inch to each dimension for size 14, two inches to each dimension for size 16, etc. Be sure to keep a pattern of the pieces for blocking purposes.

WOOL   Three-ply Persian. Use the full three plies for each thread.

OUNCES	COLORS
¾	28
½	1
¼	25
1½	40
1	2
1	24
1½	12
1	26
3	67
3	4

PREPARATION   Bind canvas with masking tape. Trace design, hem indications and dart indications on the three pieces of canvas. The tracing provided for the front is for the right front. Turn it face down to trace the left front. The tracing provided for the back is the right half of the back. Turn it face down to trace the left half of the back, making sure the center motifs are in register.

You will find it impossible to follow the outlines of the design exactly. For example, you will not be able to stitch perfect circles. Don't let it bother you, as this is intended. Stitch as close to the outlines as you can. In this design the irregularities are part of the desired effect.

I find it easiest to work with one color at a time, filling it in wherever it is indicated. For instance, I do every area of turquoise on the design before I start with another color.

Wherever possible, use the Basketweave stitch. Do *not* stitch seam allowances or dart allowances. These areas should be left unworked.

Block the three pieces to the rectangular patterns you kept of your original pieces of canvas. Block face down and steam heavily so that the canvas is good and moist. Do *not* treat with rabbit-skin glue. Allow to dry for at least 48 hours.

After the piece is blocked, machine stitch all the way around the worked area as close as possible to the needlepoint stitches. A zipper foot will allow you to stitch even closer. Be especially certain to stitch along the neck edges and armholes and inside the darts, as the seam allowances in these areas will have to be clipped later to keep the edges from puckering when the vest is assembled.

Leave ⅝ of an inch of unworked canvas around the stitched work and cut off the excess. Treat all the cut edges with Sobo glue and allow them to dry.

On your sewing machine, sew in the darts, taking one wool stitch on each side of the dart into the seam. On the back, snip up the center of the canvas taken into the dart, spread it open and glue the edges. Whip it open to the worked stitches.

With right sides facing each other, stitch side seams and shoulder seams on the sewing machine, taking two wool stitches into the seams.

Now, turn back an inch of canvas around the neck, center fronts, and bottom of the vest. (This includes the ⅝-inch seam allowance plus ⅜ inch of worked canvas.) Measure carefully, pinning as you go. Now, by hand, whip back these seams to the stitches on the back of the canvas. Do the same at the armholes, snipping the unworked canvas on armholes and neck edges where required to go around curves.

One yard of lining material will be sufficient for most sizes. I used a white, light-weight synthetic.

Cut the lining pieces from the same pattern as the vest, leaving the same seam and dart allowances.

Sew in the darts. Sew the three pieces together at side and shoulder seams with *right* sides together, and press the seams open. With wrong side of lining to wrong side of vest, pin lining seams to vest seams to hold the lining in place; then turn the raw edges of the lining toward the vest and pin them in place along the neck edges, center fronts, armholes, and bottom. As you do this, turn under just enough lining to expose the ⅜ inch of worked canvas that you turned back when you were finishing the edge of the needlepoint. (This is done so that the lining will not show on the outside of the garment.) Then slipstitch the lining to the vest.

I suggest that you spray the entire vest with Scotchgard, giving it four or five *light* applications.

PROJECT 16

Tiffany Trivet

On the tracing for this project, the solid lines outline a twelve-inch trivet. The dotted lines indicate an extension for using the design for place mats. Of course, you may adapt the design to other projects, such as a pillow or, framed, a nice spot of color in your kitchen or dining room.

#12 mono. Cut a piece approximately 14 inches square.   *CANVAS*

WOOL   Three-ply Persian. Use only two plies in each thread.

OUNCES	COLORS ILLUSTRATED
¼	44
¼	25
¾	70
¼	15
¼	42
¼	46
¼	16
¼	26
½	2
¼	43
⅛	58
1½	9

PREPARATION   For either a trivet or a place mat, allow an extra six meshes on all four sides of the design. Glue cut edges and hem for finished edges. For a pillow, allow two inches of canvas on each side of the design. Tape the edges.

STITCHING   Stitch the black "leaded" lines of the "stained glass" first. Then fill in the colored areas, using the Basketweave stitch.

BLOCKING   Block in the conventional way or use the sweater blocker on page 118.

FINISHING   For a trivet or place mat, Braid stitch all edges. For a pillow, stitch three extra rows of black on each side to be taken into the seams.

    When making a trivet you have two options. You may encase the work in lucite, as in the illustration. You can secure the lucite pieces and screws in your needlepoint shop or by writing directly to the distributor listed in project 8. Be sure to indicate that you want the twelve-inch-square trivet. The under-piece comes equipped with a hanger in case you want to hang it as a picture.

    Lay a piece of felt of an appropriate color, cut to size, on the bottom piece of lucite. Lay the needlepoint piece on top of the felt, and the top piece of lucite completes the sandwich.

Insert the screws provided, piercing the felt and the needle-point. The nuts provided are in the shape of small domes and act as little feet for the trivet.

Your second option for a trivet is to secure a twelve-inch-square cork tile. When you are using this method, it is unnecessary to line the work. Merely glue the tile to the wrong side of the work with Sobo glue. Give the surface of the trivet several coats of Scotchgard.

To use the piece as a place mat, merely line it and treat it generously with Scotchgard.

PROJECT 17

Cummerbund and Necktie

It's time now for a unisex project. The cummerbund and bow tie look great when worn by either a man or woman, or by both at the same time. For illustration, I took Alexis Smith to the theater one evening and wore my cummerbund and tie with a dinner jacket and she wore hers with a black velvet suit. I assure you that neither of us was stoned (read both ways: pelted or drunk) and, in fact, many compliments were garnered.

Cummerbund: #12 mono. A piece 7¾ inches long by 14½ inches wide.

    Tie: #14 mono. One piece 83 meshes wide by 65 meshes long.

    One piece 18 meshes wide by 51 meshes long.

Three-ply Persian. Use two plies for each thread for cummer-   *WOOL* bund and one ply for each thread for tie.

| | | | ALTERNATES | |
OUNCES	COLORS ILLUSTRATED	BLUE	GOLD	GRAY
1	70	70	70	70
¾	18	18	63	68
½	68	36	68	69

Note: The solid lines on the tracing are for the canvas for the   *PREPARATION* cummerbund and necktie. The broken lines indicate the pattern for the linings and hems.

    Trace the cummerbund on your #12 canvas and the tie on your #14 canvas. On the cummerbund leave four meshes outside the tracing on the three straight edges. Glue these edges and prepare them for finished edges, turning hems back between the third and fourth meshes. Leave the excess beyond the curved edge for blocking and turning back after the cummerbund is blocked.

    Trace the necktie on your #14 canvas. Glue all cut edges and prepare all four sides for finished edges, turning back hems between the third and fourth meshes.

Trace the center piece for the necktie on your #14 canvas and prepare all four edges for finished edges, turning hems back between the third and fourth meshes.

STITCHING Use Basketweave stitch wherever possible, filling in with Continental.

If you desire, you may overcast parts of the design with silver metallic thread as I did on the one in the illustration. I used a brand called Schurer Art 704, which is a bumpy, twisted metallic. The stitches to be overcast are obvious in the color photograph.

BLOCKING Block the cummerbund rectangle in the conventional way, face down, but do not use rabbit-skin glue. Be sure, on the finished edges, to place your pins between the exposed threads along the edge of the finished work.

Block the tie in the conventional way for finished edges, but do not treat with glue. You will find it unnecessary to block the center piece for the tie.

FINISHING Braid stitch the three straight edges of the cummerbund. Braid stitch all four edges of the tie and the center piece.

Soften the unworked canvas in the center of the tie with some cleaning fluid. Obtain some light-weight black satin. To finish the tie, cut a piece of black satin, using the broken line on the tracing as a pattern. With the wrong side of the satin to the wrong side of the tie, turn under hems and whip by hand. Gather the tie in the center with carpet thread. Wrap the center piece around these center folds and secure both ends together on the back with carpet thread. Slip a piece of 1/2-inch black elastic that is 1 1/2 inches shorter than the neck size through the center piece on the back. Secure the center of the elastic to the center piece of the tie. Turn back 1/4 inch of elastic on each end and sew a hook to one end and an eye to the other.

To finish the cummerbund, using the broken-line pattern on the tracing, cut *two* pieces of black satin.

Leaving a 1/2-inch seam allowance, cut away the excess canvas on the curved edge of the cummerbund. Glue the cut edge and turn back the seam allowance. Stitch it down to the back of the work, making sure no unworked canvas shows along the seamed edge.

Seam the two pieces of satin, right sides together, along the bottom (straight) edge. Lay the needlepoint on the satin with its bottom edge aligned with the line of stitching you have just made; be sure that the needlepoint is centered on the satin. With either chalk or pins, mark the outline of the curved edge of the cummerbund on the satin and extend the line to both ends of the satin. Remove the needlepoint and stitch the two layers of satin together along the line you have just marked. Turn the tube of satin right side out and roll the seams between your fingers and thumb until the stitching lines are exactly on the edges. Press carefully. Then center the needlepoint on the pressed satin tube and whip it down by hand.

Measure the difference between the width of the satin girdle and the waist size. Cut a piece of one-inch-wide black elastic that is 1½ inches shorter than the difference. Cut this piece in half. Turn ½ inch of satin in on each narrow end and insert a piece of elastic. Whip in by hand. Hem the free ends of the elastic and add either a buckle or hook and eye to the free ends of the elastic.

PROJECT 18

Two "Tile" Rugs

Making rugs, no matter how large, need not be a cumbersome enterprise that can only be worked at home. These "tile" rugs are made up of eleven-inch squares—small enough to take along wherever you go. And you can finish a tile in an evening or two. You'll be amazed at how quickly your rug grows. You can make it any size, as long as the length and width are multiples of twenty-two inches, merely by adding more tiles. One of the biggest advantages of these rugs is that each "tile" is blocked separately, so that when they are all put together the rug doesn't require the expensive procedure of having a large piece blocked professionally.

Use #5 rug canvas. It usually comes 40 inches wide. A 40-inch length of this width will make nine finished tiles. The blue-and-beige rug is made up of 24 tiles and requires about 3⅓ yards of canvas. The black, orange and beige rug is made up of 48 tiles and requires 6⅔ yards of canvas.

CANVAS

Use three-ply rug yarn. Amounts given are for one "tile." Multiply by the number of "tiles" you intend to use. Work with full three-ply threads.

WOOL

For Blue-and-Beige Rug

		ALTERNATES		
OUNCES	COLORS ILLUSTRATED	GREEN	GOLD	RED
¼	53 (Beige)	53	53	53
¼	66 (Lt. Blue)	42	8	15
1	32 (Med. Blue)	43	63	16
1	37 (Dark Blue)	48	64	18

This allows sufficient dark-colored wool for joining and binding.

For Black, Orange and Beige Rug

		ALTERNATES			
OUNCES	COLORS ILLUSTRATED	GREEN	BROWN	GOLD	RED
¾	53 (Beige)	53	53	53	53
¾	15 (Orange)	46	55	63	16
½	70 (Black)	70	70	70	70

This allows sufficient dark-colored wool for joining and binding.

For six-inch fringe, allow ⅔ of an ounce for each tile edge on the perimeter of the finished rug.

FRINGE

Cut canvas into squares, each side of which includes 59 meshes (double threads).

Run a thin line of Sobo glue along the double thread on each side of the square. Allow to dry.

PREPARATION

Fold back each side of the square along the fourth double thread to make hems. Be sure the holes in the turned-back hems match the holes on the face of the square.

These hems can now be sewed down by hand, using carpet thread and a backstitch within the double thread at the edge of the turnback. I have found that I can save an enormous amount of time by sewing these hems on the sewing machine if the seams are folded carefully. Set your machine for twelve stitches to the inch.

For either rug, mark off the corner squares of the design first with your indelible marker. These squares are made up of ten stitches on each side for the first rug and twelve stitches on each side for the second rug. With a ruler, using the squares as starting points, all the other lines can now be scribed. Naturally, as all stitches in the finished rug must slant in the same direction, it is not possible to draw all the tiles the same and then turn them to suit the design. It takes four "tiles" to make one motif and each must be marked according to its position in the four-tile motif. Be sure to put a color-key letter in each section of the "tile" so that you know what position of the "tile" is upright for stitching and what color goes where.

For the blue-and-beige rug, mark "tiles" as follows: B=Beige, L=Light Blue, M=Medium Blue, D=Dark Blue. This 24-tile rug requires six of each of the tiles below.

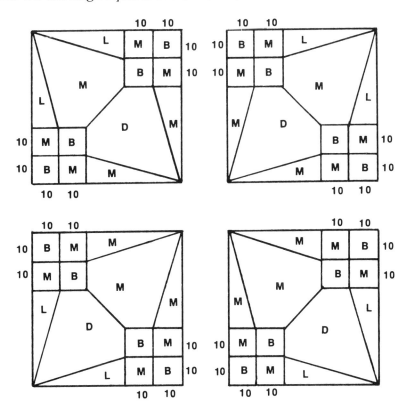

For the black, orange and beige rug, mark "tiles" as follows: B=Beige, Bl=Black, O=Orange. This 48-tile rug requires twelve of each of the tiles below.

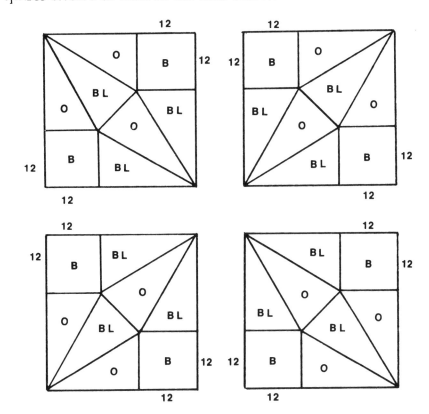

STITCHING   Work canvas with the Basketweave stitch to cause as little distortion as possible. Because of the intrinsic nature of needlepoint, it is impossible to achieve a perfectly straight diagonal line in some directions. These diagonals are worked in "steps" as illustrated in the diagram for working a diagonal line in chapter 5, but they will give the effect of a perfectly straight diagonal line when the rug is on the floor.

BLOCKING   As in all needlepoint, your finished squares will be somewhat distorted, even though they have been worked with the Basketweave stitch. They must be blocked back into perfect squares that will keep their shape. The conventional method of blocking described in chapter 6 may be used: be sure to apply rabbit-skin glue so that the squares will hold their true shape permanently.

There is another method of blocking rectangles that I find quicker and easier for this project. You can secure a sweater blocker either in a knitting shop or from a mail order catalog. The one I use is marked for blocking sweaters on one side and blocking mats on the other. It is made of fiber board with holes punched in it in parallel lines. Rust proof pins are provided that can be inserted in the board to outline many shapes of many sizes. The board I have is large enough to place sufficient pins to outline two eleven-inch squares so that two "tiles" may be blocked simultaneously. Once you have arranged the pins to the exact size of your squares, the board becomes a permanent blocker for the tiles.

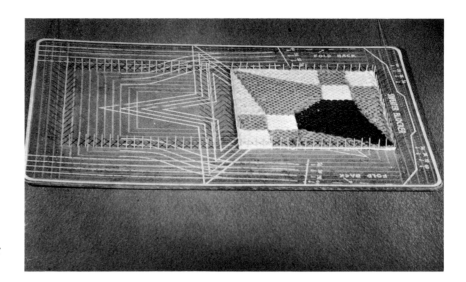

Using a sweater and mat blocker to block a "tile."

Block the "tile" face down, as you would in the conventional way. Merely slip the exposed threads along the edge of the "tile" over the pins, pulling the work back again into a perfect square. Now proceed to steam it and impregnate with rabbit-skin glue, as described in the chapter on blocking. I find it best to block each tile or couple of tiles as I finish stitching them. In this way, one or two tiles are thoroughly dry by the time I stitch a few more, and the board is free.

With the proper edges of two tiles together, hold them back to back and, with carpet thread, sew the exposed threads together with an overcast stitch, making sure you match hole for hole.

Now, starting at the left edge, work the Braid stitch over the overcast seam. In assembling, I find it best to join tiles together to make a row the full width of the rug. Then I overcast this row to the next row and Braid stitch the two rows together. Proceed as above until all rows have been added.

ASSEMBLING

The rug may be finished by merely doing a Braid stitch around all four sides (as was done with the first rug) or by adding six-inch fringe as was done on the second, using the latch-hook method described in chapter 8.

FINISHING

These rugs should be interlined with felt and lined with burlap. Felt can be found in 72-inch widths, as can burlap. Cut the felt so that it is a half-inch less than the exact length and a half-inch less than the exact width of the rug. Whip this by hand to the binding or fringe knots, being careful to keep it absolutely flat with the rug. Now cut your burlap so that it is one-and-a-half inches longer and one-and-a-half inches wider than your rug. Turn under three-quarters of an inch on each side and, by hand, whip this to the braiding or fringe knots, again being careful to keep the burlap absolutely flat with the rug.

LINING

Circular Table Cover

You have to be a little mad to undertake this project—but the end result is not only magnificent but priceless. Be warned that it will take you approximately 249 hours to stitch and the materials will cost about $300. But that's not bad when you consider that decorators charge from $1,500 to $2,000 to have one made up for you in fabric with appliquéd trim. Your finished table cover will not only be far smarter than the decorator versions, but it will improve in value as it gets older, rather than depreciate.

It is an important enough piece to design a whole room around, once you've chosen the basic color you want to use. I am using the illustrated one in a room that is primarily done in yellow and lime with accents of persimmon.

Before tackling this, be advised that it is too cumbersome to put in a bag and work on at a friend's house. It all has to be worked at home, preferably on a large table.

The cloth is designed to fit a table 27 inches high with a top measuring 24 inches in diameter.

7½ yards of #5 rug canvas—40 inches wide. *CANVAS*

Three-ply rug yarn. Use full three plies for each thread. *WOOL*

		ALTERNATES			
OUNCES	COLORS ILLUSTRATED	PINK	GREEN	BLUE	BEIGE
51	5	22	45	34	53
8	63	20	46	33	65
20	8	18	48	36	56
10	6	23	42	29	54
15	7	24	43	35	55
5	67	67	67	67	67

Tassels		ALTERNATES			
OUNCES	COLORS ILLUSTRATED	PINK	GREEN	BLUE	BEIGE
16	5	22	45	34	53
16	8	18	48	36	56
16	7	24	43	35	55

PREPARATION

Cut canvas into three pieces—each 90 inches long. Cut off selvages and glue all edges.

Baste the long sides of the three pieces together, the two side pieces overlapping the center piece by four holes of the canvas. When basting, be sure all holes and threads match exactly. Refer to grafting technique (p. 59).

When you have the three pieces basted together, find the center of the composite piece (45 inches from the top and 60 inches in from the sides). Using this point as center, scribe a circle 24 inches in diameter. (Using a marker tied to a piece of string 12 inches long will give you the proper radius and is an easy way of scribing the circle.)

Lay the pattern for this project under the canvas, matching the curve at the top (smaller end) to the circle you've scribed. Mark the edges of the pattern on your circle and mark the edges at the bottom of the pattern as registry marks.

Trace the pattern on your canvas. Now move the pattern to the right, matching registry marks, and trace the pattern again, each time marking your registry points.

Keep moving the pattern to the right and tracing, each time making sure the top curve registers perfectly with your circle and with your registry marks, until the entire design is traced onto your canvas, making a perfect circle.

Take out your bastings and work each of the three pieces separately.

STITCHING

Wherever possible, use the Basketweave stitch. Stitch the entire design and background on each of the three pieces *except* for the four holes which overlap when the three pieces are put together. As each motif will be on a different grain of the canvas, you will not be able to stitch each one the same. Outlines will vary from "pineapple" to "pineapple" and from "swag" to "swag." Don't let this worry you. Just follow the traced design as closely as you can. The variations will not be apparent in the finished cloth.

Block each of the three pieces separately before assembling. *BLOCKING*
You will need a wooden surface or piece of plywood about
100 inches long by 50 inches wide to block each rectangle. On
your blocking surface, mark a rectangle 90 inches by 40 inches
and block each of the three pieces to these perimeters. Block
in the prescribed way, face down, giving the back a light coat-
ing of rabbit-skin glue.

After each of the three rectangles has been blocked, carefully *ASSEMBLING*
sew them together again with carpet thread, matching hole for
hole, thread for thread.

Using the proper colors of wools, needlepoint over the
joins, stitching as you would if it were a single piece.

Scribe a circle two inches below the finished work. Cut away *FINISHING*
the excess canvas up to this mark—in other words, you are
leaving two inches of unworked canvas to be used as a hem.

Turn up the unworked canvas to the back and stitch to
the back of the worked canvas, making small gussets to accommodate the curve.

Use 14-inch lengths of yarn to make the tassels in order to end *TASSELS*
up with a finished tassel 6½ inches long. I made my tassels by
mixing twenty pieces of #5, the background color, with ten
pieces of #8 and ten pieces of #7.

Follow the instructions in chapter 8 for making tassels,
except, instead of pulling the ends of the binding yarn up
through the top of the tassel, tie a knot and let the ends hang
free.

Where the bottom "drapery" in the design "gathers,"
pull the two threads at the top of the tassel through the work
and tie together on the back of the cloth.

Now pull the two ends of the binding yarn through the
work to the wrong side and tie these together. Your tassel is
now secured in two places.

At your notions store buy sixteen 1¼ ounce weights. If they *WEIGHTS*
only carry lighter ones, use enough at each place to total 1¼
ounces.

On the back of the cloth sew a weight behind each tassel, about 1½ inches from the bottom of the cloth. This will make your cloth hang in even folds.

LINING   Use unbleached muslin or a light-weight synthetic. Sew a sufficient number of widths together to make a piece 90 by 120 inches. Lay your finished cover on the lining and scribe a circle on the lining two inches larger than the table cover. With wrong side of lining to wrong side of cover, turn scam allowance of lining under and whip to cover, being sure to keep both pieces perfectly flat so you do not "pull up" the cover with the lining.

NOTE   A piece of glass twenty-four inches in circumference with a polished edge laid on top of the table over the cover will save the work from spills and stains.

PROJECT 20

Shell Tiles

Four different shell designs are provided on six-inch "tiles."
In the illustration they are used to decorate the four sides of a
clear plastic box. However, they may be used individually for
trivets or combined to make a pillow. The tracings of the shells
themselves may be used individually or in combination to add
to other designs.

#8/16 penelope. About a 7½-inch square for each "tile."   CANVAS

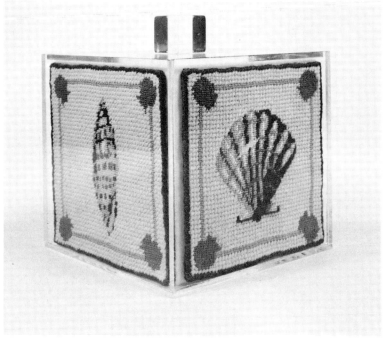

WOOL   Three-ply Persian. Use only one ply for each thread for everything except the background. Use the full three plies for the
background. Amounts given are enough to work all four tiles.

OUNCES	COLORS ILLUSTRATED
¼	59
⅛	60
¼	62
¼	19
⅛	21
½	67
2	45

PREPARATION   Cut canvas squares, allowing four extra meshes on each side
beyond the perimeter of the tile. Glue all edges and hem all
four sides for finished edges.

STITCHING   Stitch the shell, the border and corner motifs in petit point,
using one ply for each thread. Stitch the background, in gros

point, using the Basketweave stitch, with the full three plies for each thread.

Block to your paper pattern in the conventional way for a finished edge, being sure to place your pins between the finished work and the exposed mesh.

BLOCKING

Braid stitch each edge of each square, using two plies for each thread of color #62.

FINISHING

You may obtain the plastic box that I have illustrated in your needlepoint shop. It is especially made to receive needlepoint. If your shop doesn't carry it, you may order it directly from the same distributor given in project 8. It's called, unfortunately, a Goody Box.

If you wish to use the tiles as trivets, attach them to squares of cork tile with Sobo glue. If you use them in this way, be sure to spray them several times with Scotchgard.

The tiles may also be used to decorate wooden boxes. Merely apply with Sobo glue.